AN INTRO
FEMINISM A

Feminist thinking constitutes a lively, oppositional and energizing force at the centre of the theatre academy. Although a
relatively new field of study, its dynamic impact is changing the
way in which theatre is taught and practised. *An Introduction to
Feminism and Theatre* is an accessible and intelligent overview of
feminist theory, plays, practitioners and practice, all of which are
changing the perception of theatre as a whole.

An Introduction to Feminism and Theatre is split into two sections.
In the first part the reader is guided through the key feminist
concepts and methodological practices relevant to the historical,
theoretical and practical study of theatre. Aston discusses how
feminist theatre history has re-examined and changed the theatrical canon, surveys the European context of French feminist
theory and theatre, and introduces recent theoretical thinking
about gender and performance practice. The second section consists of case studies which illustrate the various strands of theoretical debate.

This book will be essential reading for anyone needing a clear and
lucid guide to an increasingly important and dynamic force in
theatre.

Elaine Aston is Lecturer in Theatre Studies at the University of
Loughborough. She has published extensively on historical and
contemporary aspects of feminist theatre. Her publications in-
clude a full-length study of Sarah Bernhardt (1989) and *Theatre as
Sign-System* (with George Savona, 1991). She is also co-editor, with
G. Griffin, of two volumes of plays performed by the Women's
Theatre Group (*Herstory I and II, 1991*).

AN
INTRODUCTION
TO FEMINISM
AND THEATRE

Elaine Aston

London and New York

First published 1995
by Routledge
11 New Fetter Lane, London EC4P 4EE

Transferred to Digital Printing 2003

Simultaneously published in the USA and Canada
by Routledge
29 West 35th Street, New York, NY 10001

Typeset in Palatino by
Ponting–Green Publishing Services,
Chesham, Buckinghamshire

British Library Cataloguing in Publication Data
A catalogue record for this book is available from
the British Library

Library of Congress Cataloging in Publication Data
Aston, Elaine
An introduction to feminism and theatre/Elaine Aston.
p.   cm.
Includes bibliographical references and index.
1. Feminism and theater.   2.Feminist theater.
3. Women in the theater.   I. Title.
PN1590.W64A88   1994
792'.082–dc20   94–12202

ISBN 0–415–08768–6 (hbk)
ISBN 0–415–08769–4 (pbk)

Printed and bound by Antony Rowe Ltd, Eastbourne

To my daughter Magdalene,
with love

CONTENTS

CONTENTS

ACKNOWLEDGEMENTS

Extracts from the poems 'i is a long married woman', 'One Continent/To Another', 'Skin Teeth', and 'Nanny' were taken from the collection, *i is a long memoried woman*, printed with permission of the publishers. Copyright 1983, 1990 Karnak House.

I am grateful to Sue Roe for asking me to contribute this volume to her series. I should also like to thank all of the women practitioners who have accepted invitations to Loughborough and shared their creativity through workshops, performances, readings, and lectures. In particular, I should like to thank Cristina Castrillo and Jill Greenhalgh for their inspiration. My thanks go also to the company members of women's theatre groups who spared some of their valuable time to be interviewed about their work in 1989 and 1990.

During my years of teaching women's theatre courses I have continued to learn from the students in my seminars and workshops. I should especially like to thank the women in the 1992–3 group who helped me think through ideas and material for this study. A special thank you to Lisa Rogers and Kirsti Sandom who created an earlier performed version of the case study in Chapter 11 at the 'Romantic Boundaries' Conference, Sheffield, 1993.

Finally, I wish to thank my mother for her constant encouragement and help with childcare, and Ian Clarke for his continuing support and friendship.

Elaine Aston
Loughborough

1

BACKGROUND
Feminism and theatre studies

INTRODUCTION

In recent years feminism has proved, and is still proving, a vital
and energizing challenge to the male bias of teaching and research
across a wide range of academic disciplines. In the theatre academy,
more commonly termed theatre studies, the impact of feminism
has been felt at a much later stage than in its 'sister' disciplines,
such as English studies. This is largely due to the way in which
theatre studies as a discipline is itself a relatively new phenomenon: the first British university drama department opened at
Bristol as late as 1947 (see Barker 1994; on earlier pioneering efforts
see Thomson 1991; for American details see Case 1990: 2, n.2). In
general, drama departments evolved out of English departments
which were (and in many instances still are) concerned with the
teaching of plays as dramatic literature. The brief history of the
discipline is therefore a troubled one in terms of its fight for
autonomy and the recognition of its practices, which it is still in the
process of defining (see Reinelt and Roach 1992: 5).

Centrally, however, theatre studies set out to re-frame the study
of drama as the study of theatre in its historical, theoretical, and
practical contexts. Each of these three key areas has undergone
conceptual and methodological shifts in the move towards a 'new'
theorized field of theatre study. The importance of feminism in
recent thinking about theatre history, theory, and practice is considerable. This current study sets out to demonstrate its importance
through a survey of the feminist project(s) in theatre studies. The
volume is offered as an accessible and practical guide to students
of theatre desirous of understanding the 'stages' in feminism, and,
hopefully, of making their own feminist interventions in the field.

Feminism and theatre history

Writing on the growth of theatre studies in the American context, feminist theatre academic Sue-Ellen Case comments, 'as the study of theatre within theatre departments developed, it was dominated by the history of theatre, rather than its criticism' (1990: 2). This, on both sides of the Atlantic, was a consequence of the way in which theatre studies sought to re-locate the study of plays within their historico-theatrical contexts. Theatre, studied as dramatic literature in English departments, had been divorced from the context of its production. Theatre studies, however, began to examine the history of playing spaces, performance conditions, audience compositions, and the various artistic, social, and political functions assigned to theatre at different times. In this context, playtexts themselves, once 'read' as theatrical as opposed to dramatic texts, were seen to contain important information about aspects of their contemporary staging.

Moreover, a broad shift in critical thinking from a concern with the interiority of a text to the material concerns of its production called for a re-evaluation of the binary 'high' and 'low' culture divide. The impact of this on the study of theatre history resulted in the consideration of historical stages which had previously not been deemed worthy of study, on the grounds that they had no 'great' dramatic literature to offer (for example, the popular traditions of the nineteenth-century British stage). Examining the material conditions of theatre as a cultural form, a practice recognized as cultural materialism, furthered an understanding of the theatrical and social conditioning of a cultural past to be seen as a continuum of a materially-conditioned cultural present.

Understanding the cultural and material conditions of theatre past (and present) is central to a feminist re-framing of theatre history, which has its own questions to ask about how and why women's work has been 'hidden' or marginalized. Writing in 1981, Nancy Reinhardt observes that 'women's studies in theatre criticism . . . is relatively new and in theatre history only just beginning' (25). She makes the following suggestions for the theatre historian:

> How might feminist thinking be applied to the standard non-verbal (pictorial) evidence that historians use to construct theories about past production? The theatre historian should re-examine this historical evidence with a lens which focuses

more closely on the position of women in productions of earlier centuries. The dominant *public* action both on the stage and in the audience stresses a male world in which women are either kept to the sides, in recesses, or are placed on display for the male viewer.

(ibid.: 28–9)

By 1985, the year of the first British academic women's theatre conference held at Warwick University, a 'feminist thinking', or rather re-thinking, of theatre history was shown to be well underway (see end of bibliography for full details of major national British women's theatre conferences in higher education institutions). Different periods of theatre history from the Renaissance to the nineteenth century were re-examined by feminist approaches. The methodologies used to frame the historical material were a mixture of the 'old' and the 'new'. On the traditional side these included the 'images of women in male-authored drama approach' derived from feminist literary studies (see next section for further comment), and the empirical research of under/non-documented work by women in theatre. The conference also showed feminist intervention in more recent theoretical positions used to re-frame theatre history: a feminist appropriation of semiotics (see next section for explanation and details) critiqued the images of women in nineteenth-century theatre; feminist–cultural–materialist analysis alienated the representation of women (by men) on the Renaissance stage.

When Manchester University hosted a second major feminist theatre history conference in 1989, focusing specifically on the late nineteenth- and early twentieth-century British stages, it demonstrated that there was now an established and growing body of feminist historico-revisionist activity in the field of theatre studies. The 'new direction' in theatre history was exposing the history of male domination of the stage and recovering women's performance which, like so much of women's culture, had been 'hidden' and silenced by a body of conservative, male criticism.

Feminist critical theory and theatre

Case's comment, cited above, on the emphasis of theatre history within the theatre academy, is presented in her introduction to *Performing Feminisms: Feminist Critical Theory and Theatre*, where she outlines the resistance from theatre historians to the study of 'new' critical theory in theatre studies. She explains how both she and Timothy Murray, as editors of the American *Theatre Journal* in the 1980s, were criticized for publishing articles both specifically on 'the feminist critique in theatre studies', and generally on 'critical theory in theatre studies' (1990: 1). As Case explains in a footnote to her introduction:

> As editors of the journal, Murray and I were severely criticized for the predominance of articles that incorporated theory and specifically political theory into their content. This move was interpreted as a move away from what was perceived as the center of theatre studies – the traditional uses of theatre history. This so-called schism between theory and history beleaguered the journal, its parent organisation and theatre departments during the decade of the 1980s.
>
> (ibid.)

Despite resistance from within the theatre academy, critical theory has continued to gain ground. As Reinelt and Roach explain in the introduction to *Critical Theory and Performance*, 'there has been a theory explosion, and it has had important consequences for both theatre studies and other humanities as well' (1992: 4). This controversial 'theory explosion', both in general terms and specifically in relation to feminism, may again be traced to the evolution of theatre studies as a discipline.

Although setting a practical agenda to the study of drama, theatre studies continued to rely heavily on the published playtext. However, in order to avoid the conventional 'plays-as-dramatic-literature' approach as practised in English studies, it looked for new ways of 'reading' texts. Central to these was and is the field of theatre semiotics. Semiotics offered an understanding of the theatrical text as a sign-system, and, moreover, provided a 'language' for the study of plays in performance. In the 1980s, the British theatre journal *Theatre Quarterly* (subsequently *New Theatre Quarterly*) published articles on theatre and semiotic theory (for examples see Bassnett 1980; Pavis 1985), although this semiotic 'explosion' of the 1980s also met with marked critical hostility (see Aston and Savona 1991: 1). In addition to semiotics, there were several other spheres of critical theory in the 1980s which provided important frameworks and methodologies for the study of plays and performance. The field of theatre connected with disciplines such as anthropology, sociology, and psychoanalysis. It was re-examined within the contexts of post-structuralism, post-modernism, and deconstruction; was cross-examined by the new historians, Marxist scholars, cultural materialists, and by the theory and practice of feminism(s).

As theatre studies was a late developer and the impact of feminism came much later than in other studies, feminist critical theory in theatre began by 'borrowing' from feminist projects in related disciplines. For example, pioneering feminist approaches to literature in English studies had established the deconstructive approaches to male-authored images of women in the canon of 'classics'. Feminist theatre scholarship was subsequently able to draw on this work to develop a conceptual and methodological framework for critiquing how women are 'imaged' in dramatic texts. Unlike its literary 'sister', however, the feminist study of theatre had not only to 'resist' or re-read the written text, but also needed to find ways of 'reading' the performance context. Theatre studies looked to film and media studies where feminist scholarship focused on the construction of 'woman' as sign: an approach in which feminism, psychoanalysis, and semiotics was and is being used to understand how women are represented in cinematic texts and other cultural contexts.

The pioneering emphasis on understanding the construction of 'woman' as sign in mainstream (male) production contexts gradually gave way, however, to a field more centrally concerned with the theory and practice of women's texts and performance contexts. Theatre scholarship in America has been the pioneering, driving force behind the theorizations of feminist theatre. Not only did *Theatre Journal* raise the profile of feminist critical theory and theatre under Case's committed and admirable editorship, but the early 1980s also saw the founding of the journal *Women and Performance*, subtitled *A Journal of Feminist Theory* (for details and discussion see Dolan 1989a). Furthermore, in 1980 the Women's Theatre Program was established as a sub-group of the American Theatre Association (now American Theatre in Higher Education). The inception of the WTP meant that it was possible to hold a WTP conference before each of the ATA's annual 'main' conventions (see Dolan 1984: 5). As Jill Dolan, reporting on the WTP conference in 1983, argues, 'feminist theatre needs a national platform like the WTP to communicate its theory and work on a wider scale' (1984: 6).

5

Whilst the WTP offers a 'national platform' for women's theatre in America, national conference networking in Britain has had to rely on the energies of individual women to create forums for discussion. Although slower to develop, feminist critical theory and theatre has begun to play a more central role in the British theatre academy. In 1989 Warwick's newly formed *Women and Theatre Newsletter* (now a series of Occasional Papers) provided details of women's theatre options running in fifteen institutions of Higher Education. Such courses were framed by the growing field of feminist critical theory used to explicate textual and performance analysis. By the time of the next Warwick conference in 1990, it was evident that there was a young generation of British feminist theatre scholars whose diverse paths of enquiry shared the commmon ground of wanting to understand and to theorize women's creativity in theatre.

Feminism and theatrical practice/s

In so critical a period as today, those women who work in the theatre try, as a transitory step, to reduce the participation of men in their work. They prefer to work on texts *written* by women, or write or adapt texts themselves . . . These women even prefer to create their own settings, so that the male imagination cannot sneak back in with flamboyantly erected stage images that silently glorify the phallus.

(Pasquier 1986: 197)

Feminist theorization of stage practice has been critical of those realist traditions of performance which work in tandem with dominant and oppressive representations of gender, and 'glorify the phallus' centre stage. In terms of contemporary theatrical practice, theatre studies remains centrally informed by the actor training programmes of Stanislavski and Brecht: between the art of 'becoming' the character and the work of demonstration. As feminism looked to a theatrical practice rooted in a desire for political change it rejected the Stanislavski-based legacy and found an ally in Brecht – not to adopt his performance methods, but to engage them in the staging of a feminist politics and aesthetics.

Moreover, as theatre studies, as conceived in its university context, had not set out to provide professional training for its students, it suffered from a gap between the academic context of its work and the work of professional theatre practitioners. Recognizing that contact with professional feminist practice is necessary if theatre studies is to participate in the challenge to the 'male imagination' which dominates the stage, feminist theatre practice has sought to bridge the gap between the academy and the profession. In America the WTP conferences provide a forum for bringing feminist academics and practitioners together (see Dolan 1984). In Britain the narrowing of the gap between the professional and the academic has been evidenced in the most recent of the women's theatre conferences. In 1991 the Lough-borough conference was led by speakers and workshop leaders who were all professional women practitioners: directors, play-wrights, and performers. At Warwick in 1992 the roundtable discussion on the figure of Medea, which concluded the confer-ence, consisted almost entirely of professional participants (with only Susan Bassnett as Chair, and myself as participant, coming from an academic context). Given that the early women's theatre conferences were almost entirely academic, in terms of speakers and audiences, this reversal is indicative of the extent to which theatrical practice is moving to the centre of feminist theatre studies.

THE PROJECT

My main objective in this study is, as I have stated, to offer an accessible overview of how and why feminism has been important to theatre studies, and the 'stages' of its impact on the discipline. Thus far, the field has been predominantly (although not exclus-ively) pioneered by American feminist theatre scholarship. The documentation and analysis of feminist theatre groups has been the subject of several full-length American studies (for examples see Brown 1979; Leavitt 1980; Natalle 1985). Important surveyings of the field have been published by feminist theatre scholars Keyssar (1984), Case (1988), and Dolan (1988). The American theatrical canon has been challenged in two volumes edited by Schlueter (1989; 1990). The advances made in the American sphere of feminist critical theory and theatre (as previously discussed) are evidenced in the recent publication of collections of essays edited by Hart (1989) and Case (1990). The work of the American feminist theatre scholars has, therefore, raised the profile of feminist practitioners working in a variety of performance contexts, and has, for example, given attention to American lesbian performers, female performance artists, the theatre created by women of colour, etc.

In a British context important early surveys include Itzin's sampling of feminist theatre (1980), and Wandor (1986), though these are factual and descriptive rather than analytical. Goodman's recent study (1993a) offers a more detailed sourcebook of contemporary feminist theatres. However, whilst stronger in the context of feminist theatre history (for examples see Gardner and Rutherford 1992; Howe 1992), the British field remains weak in the areas of feminist critical theory and theatrical practice. This present study, therefore, seeks to strengthen these aspects of the field through a transatlantic surveying of American feminist theatre scholarship, in conjunction with a high profiling of feminist practitioners and playwrights in a British context.

Feminism or feminisms? A note on terminology

Within the scope of this project there is not the space to devote chapters to defining feminism, or indeed defining theatre. Dolan, in the introduction to her study of feminism and theatre, usefully states that 'feminism begins with a keen awareness of exclusion from male cultural, social, sexual, political, and intellectual discourse. It is a critique of prevailing social conditions that formulate women's position as outside of dominant male discourse' (1988: 3). Dolan continues, however, by stating that 'the routes feminism takes to redress the fact of male dominance . . . are varied', and that consequently 'feminism has in fact given way more precisely to feminisms' (ibid.). This present study works from the premise that the defining discourse of feminism is its critique of the 'dominant male discourse', and is specifically concerned with the identification and analysis of the feminist discourse in theatre. Yet it is also concerned with charting the different 'routes' feminism has travelled in theatre studies.

In particular, the study uses the three dominant feminist positions as they are recognized in British and American contexts as a frame of reference: bourgeois, radical, and materialist. Briefly, bourgeois or liberal feminism proposes the amelioration of women's position in society without any radical change to its political, economic, or social structures, e.g. through legislative reform. Radical feminism locates the oppression of women in the patriarchal domination of women by men, and advocates the abolition of the man-made structures which reinforce gender-based inequality. (Radical feminism has more recently been termed cultural feminism, especially in American contexts. For discussion on this point see Dolan 1988: 5–6.) Materialist feminism has now been widely adopted as the nomenclature for the theoretical position which in the 1970s was labelled as Marxist or socialist feminism. This position critiques the historical and material conditions of class, race, and gender oppression, and demands the radical transformation of social structures. (For an early and accessible introduction to these three feminisms see Beechy 1982; for an overview of their evolution linked to a theatrical context see Dolan 1988: Chapter 1). As the study examines these different feminist dynamics in the context of theatre, it charts not only the challenge which feminist theatre poses to the discourse of mainstream (male) theatre, but the dialectics of its own self-reflexive critique: from feminism to feminisms; from feminist theatre to feminist theatres.

The structure

The study is organized into two main parts: Part One surveys feminist approaches to the history, theory, and practice of theatre; Part Two is devoted to case studies which engage in the critical practice of theories and methodologies presented in Part One. As an alternative to a chapter-by-chapter approach, the reader may find it useful to combine a 'theory' chapter with a case study (relevant connections and cross-referencings are signalled in the text).

Part One opens with a chapter on feminism and theatre history which identifies the ways in which feminist theatre scholarship has critiqued the 'canon' and discovered a 'lost' tradition of women's theatre. Chapter 3 examines the impact of feminist theories of representation on the field of theatre. It foregrounds the field of psychosemiotics: a mixing of Lacanian psychoanalysis, semiotics, and feminism pioneered by British and American film and media studies, and, as indicated, more recently taken up by feminist theatre studies. The issue of subject positioning is pursued in Chapter 4 in the European context of French feminist theory and its key exponents Hélène Cixous, Luce Irigaray, and Julia Kristeva. The chapter focuses on the different ways in which 'woman's' position as 'Other' and non-speaking subject is critiqued through this framework, and highlights the importance of 'writing the body' which feminist theatre studies has derived from this theoretical field. Chapter 5 surveys the ways in which feminism has impacted on theatrical practice. It identifies the theory and practice of the feminist groups emerging in Britain and America in the 1970s, and examines the evolution of this first wave of feminist theatrical activity in relation to the three dominant feminist positions: bourgeois, radical/cultural, and socialist/materialist. Chapter 6 in Case's full-length study *Feminism and Theatre* (1988) introduces the under-documented field of 'Women of Colour and Theatre' in America. Chapter 6 in this study attempts a similar project from this side of the Atlantic: presenting voices from Black women's theatre in Britain, identifying their marginal position in relation to mainstream, white, feminist theatre, and the re-shaping of feminist theory and theatrical practice which their marginality demands. Chapter 7 examines the more recent theoretical thinking about gender and the challenge which this poses to the assumption of a stable and unified subject of feminism. In particular, Chapter 7 highlights the theory and practice of lesbian theatre in American and British contexts.

In Part Two, Chapter 8, the case study of Susan Glaspell illustrates the male bias of criticism which constructs the 'canon', and details how women dramatists 'disappear' from theatre history. Chapter 9, the case study 'Bodily Harm', examines three plays – *Steaming* (Nell Dunn), *Heresies* (Deborah Levy), and *Masterpieces* (Sarah Daniels) – to explore different feminist theories through the theatre texts. The 'bodily harm' focus examines the representation of the female body as a site/sight of male violence, and returns to a number of the issues concerning the representation of women as subjects, detailed in Part One. Chapter 10, 'Colonial Landscapes', is a case study of the videotext *i is a long memoried woman*, based on the collection of poems by Grace Nichols. This study is designed to explore and complement the issues of race and gender raised in Chapter 6.

Whereas in Part One the study focuses on feminist concepts and methodological approaches to theatre, and the case studies to date explore feminist theoretical positions explicated through texts and performance contexts, the final case study makes a slightly different proposal which acts as a conclusion to the volume. Chapter 11 takes two plays which perform a feminist

10

criticism of Romanticism: *Blood and Ice* (Liz Lochhead) and *Breathless* (April de Angelis), and considers the 'ways of seeing' which feminist theatre has to offer women's studies. The concept of enacting feminist criticism on/through the body is presented as a performative methodology which women's studies, in the future, may look to as a valuable source of critical practice.

Part I

FEMINIST APPROACHES TO THEATRE

2

FINDING A TRADITION
Feminism and theatre history

'HIDDEN FROM HISTORY'

'My four-million-year-old ancestor opened its eyes . . . and stood up . . . And I realised that what I had found was a woman', says Molly, the archaeologist in Bryony Lavery's play *Origin of the Species* (1987: 67). The discovery that her ancestor is female enables Molly to re-think the destructive man-made history of the human race which has brought the 'species' to the point of extinction. Lavery's interrogative approach to the 'origin of the species' is emblematic of the ways in which women, in the wake of the Liberation Movement in the late 1960s and 1970s, began to question representations of the past, and to discover how they had been 'hidden from history' (see Rowbotham 1973).

The feminist concept of women 'hidden from history' impacted on literary criticism in two ways. First, it motivated feminist critics to understand how and why women, like Molly's ancestor, had been buried by man-made history, and, second, it initiated the recovery of their 'lost' female ancestors. In literary criticism this involved explicating how women had been oppressively represented by men in literature (see Millett 1977 [1969]), and finding a tradition of women's writing (see Moers 1976). The task of finding a tradition of women's writing, or of re-discovering women's poetry (see Bernikow 1979 [1974]), was not so readily fulfilled when feminism intervened in the history of theatre. In her introduction to the American anthology of contemporary plays by women, playwright Honor Moore argued that the way that men had prevented women from participating in theatre was 'responsible for the lack of a female tradition in playwrighting similar to that which exists in both fiction and poetry' (1977: xiv). Moore

15

offered a potted history of women in theatre, mostly based on information taken from what is still one of the few full-length studies in this field – Rosamund Gilder's *Enter the Actress* (1931) – by way of introducing a contemporary 'tradition' of plays by women. It was not strictly speaking the case, however, that there was a 'lack of a female tradition' in the theatre as Moore argued; rather it was the relative difficulty of finding it, compared to the feminist recovery of poetry and prose authored by women.

Feminist intervention in the study of theatre history has critiqued the male exclusion of women from theatre which Moore identified, and attempted to find its own female tradition. This chapter will examine how feminism has re-charted theatre history through these two routes.

DECONSTRUCTING THE CANON

An analogous approach to the re-reading of male-made images of women, pioneered by Kate Millett in the context of literary criticism, began in theatre studies with the development of feminist approaches to the 'classic' periods of Western theatre history which, by definition, excluded women. The critical apparatus surrounding the canon and the definition of 'great' or 'classic' literature was no longer considered to be value-free, but was seen as part of the patriarchal value-system governing society and its cultural production. It critiqued, for example, those definitions of 'greatness' which relied on the appeal to the 'universal', or to 'every*man*' (most frequently cited in the context of Shakespeare).

Although the British and American male-made 'image' strands of feminist literary theory moved rapidly on to a more woman-authored line of enquiry, they have sustained a longer critical history in the context of theatre. This is because image-based methodologies have evolved into more sophisticated structuralist and semiotic lines of enquiry generated through the understanding of theatre as a sign-system. Within this context, a more highly complex method of reading theatre from an image base has developed, which, in turn, has been appropriated by feminism to re-read the gender bias of the canon. In terms of those 'classic' periods of theatre, for example, where women have been absent from the stage, it has been possible to understand how the female has been constructed as a man-made sign in her absence. Two 'classic' periods in the Western theatrical canon which have been the object of feminist deconstructive activity of this kind are the Greek and the Elizabethan stages.

Feminism and Greek theatre

Until comparatively recently Greek theatre was generally taught and studied as a branch of literature. The plays were offered in educational contexts as drama to be read, but not seen. Gradually, however, an understanding of the plays as plays, and an examination of the 'visual dimension' of Greek drama superseded the literary approach (see Taplin 1985 [1978]). The new focus was on performance conditions and performance action. Attention was paid to the possible configurations of actors on stage, the choreography of the chorus, the costuming, the wearing of masks, etc., and how these constituted a conventionalized style of theatre which operated self-referentially as a sign-system.

Feminist theatre scholarship could, in turn, make use of this kind of theatrical detail to understand how the sign of the female was constructed in a performance context:

> How does the male actor signal to the audience that he is playing a female character? Besides wearing the female costume (with short tunic) and the female mask (with long hair), he might have indicated gender through gesture, movement and intonation.
>
> (Case 1988: 11)

An understanding of how gender might be visually, gesturally, etc. signed on the stage, may then be set against a feminist reading of the texts (see Case on the *Orestia* (1988: 12–15); Ferris on Aristophanes (1990: 20–30)), which reveals the silencing of women both in the theatre and in society at large. Critical insights into how exactly gender was encoded and what the gestic style of performance consisted of can only be speculative, though it can be argued with certainty that 'the classical plays and theatrical conventions . . . be regarded as allies in the project of suppressing actual women and replacing them with the masks of patriarchal production' (Case 1985: 318).

Furthermore, in the texts of the plays out of which the performance conventions are read, those moments where the action deictically highlights ('points to') gender as a fictive construct offer tangible demonstration of the absence of women from the

17

stage and the ideological implications of this. In a commentary on Euripides's *Alcestis* (a woman who consents to sacrifice her own life to save her husband's), Bassi observes that the 'language used to describe' Alcestis 'and which she uses herself, points to the presence of the male actor behind the female *persona*; of the false image which that *persona* presents' (1989: 27). Her argument concludes: 'the actor playing his female role overtly refers to the absence of the actress, and the tragic stage simultaneously becomes a commentary on itself and on the status of the female in fifth-century Athens' (ibid.). Case offers more detail on what the female 'status' was by overviewing the increasing subordination of Athenian women as a result of legislative and economic practices which were then reflected in the cultural practices of society, such as theatre. She summarizes:

> In each of the cultures which has produced 'classics' for the stage (not only the Athenian, but the Roman, and the Elizabethan) women were denied access to the stage and to legal and economic enfranchisement. These same production values are embedded in the texts of these periods. Female characters are derived from the absence of actual women on the stage and from the reasons for their absence. Each culture which valorizes the reproduction of those 'classic' texts actively participates in the same patriarchal subtext which created those female characters as 'Woman.'
>
> (1985: 322)

This point is underlined by looking briefly at a modern feminist re-inscription of Greek theatre: Wertenbaker's *The Love of the Nightingale* (1989). *The Love of the Nightingale* performs a feminist critique of the theatrical conventions and ideological concerns of Greek theatre, culture, and society. The interests of two royal sisters, Procne and Philomele, played by two *real* women, are placed centre stage. Athenian society which condoned rape (Agamemnon's rape of Cassandra), was willing to sacrifice its daughters (Agamemnon's sacrifice of Iphigenia), and punish those women who transgressed its orders (Phaedra, Medea, or Clytemnestra), is subjected to feminist scrutiny. The signs of masculinity dominant in Greek theatre such as the phallus, valiant soldier, or conquering hero, are parodied. The dramatization of the rape and silencing of Philomele (her tongue is cut out by her rapist) is critically alienated as paradigmatic of the violent silencing of women in Greek theatre, and in their descendents: male-authored representations of women on the Western stage.

Feminism and Shakespeare

The position of Shakespeare in the national and international canon of 'great' theatre has inevitably attracted the interest, and indeed wrath, of feminist scholarship. One conciliatory line of feminist critical enquiry has been to re-read Shakespeare against the traditionally received images of women in the plays. Juliet Dusinberre is one of the early exponents of this approach. She argues for the improvement of women's position in the Renaissance period, and for the mirroring of this advancement in the work of the dramatist, to support her claims for 'Shakespeare's modernity in his treatment of women' and the thrust of the drama 'from 1590 to 1625' as 'feminist in sympathy' (1975: 5). Subsequent feminist criticism has challenged both of these claims, though the 'Shakespeare-as-feminist-in-sympathy' approach has been a dominant strand of text-orientated commentaries of feminist literary theory. As Case comments:

> most of these works, concentrating on the images of independent women in the comedies and contrasting them with the negative images of women in the tragedies, characterise Shakespeare's portrayals of women as ahead of his time, or the best of his time.

> (1988: 25)

During the 1980s radical-feminist approaches to Shakespeare's female and male characters became entrenched in essentialist re-readings of gender: what is female is pre-determined by the principle of what is male. Best-selling author Marilyn French brought the popular face of feminism to Shakespeare in a study which applied the 'dividing experience' of 'gender principles' to Shakespeare: 'In literature . . . males act out the human role, erring and correcting, experiencing the gamut of emotion and behavior, while females act out the type, standing as static poles in human (male) experience' (1983 [1981]: 26). French examined the binary movement of 'masculinity' and 'femininity' throughout the different dramatic genres in the Shakespeare canon, but the proposed radical revisioning of the 'great' dramatist was severely flawed by the essentialist view of gender which underpinned the theoretical and critical apparatus of the project.

Linda Bamber's 'study òf gender and genre in Shakespeare' similarly proposed a model of gender in which 'the Self is masculine . . . in Shakespearean tragedy, and women are Other' (1982: 9). Although there is no 'Self' for the female reader to identify with, the idea is that she may be able to position herself with the 'feminine Other' created out of a composite picture of all the women's roles in the tragedy. 'Only when I refuse the role of the Other altogether', Bamber concludes in an essay on the woman reader and *King Lear*:

> only when nothing will satisfy but a female version of the Self, do I refuse to shelter the female portion of my identity with Shakespeare's women. At that point, if I'm smart, I take a break from Shakespeare and pick up *Middlemarch*.
>
> (1986: 300)

Although the notion of re-thinking Shakespeare's women as 'Other' is subversive in terms of traditional readings of Shakespeare (which assume the reader to be every*man* identifying with Lear), it is not possible, as Kathleen Mcluskie argues, for feminism to 'simply take "the woman's part" when that part has been so morally loaded and theatrically circumscribed' (1985: 102). Mcluskie further highlights the dangers of putting down *King Lear* in favour of *Middlemarch*:

> Nor is any purpose served by merely denouncing the text's misogyny, for *King Lear's* position at the centre of the Shakespeare canon is assured by its continual reproduction in education and the theatre and is unlikely to be shifted by feminist sabre-rattling.
>
> (ibid.)

Instead, Mcluskie proposes a feminist–cultural–materialist analysis which requires an understanding of 'the contradictions of contemporary ideology and practice' in which the text was produced (104), based on the assumption that such 'contradictions' will be reflected in the text. This is radically different to Dusinberre's 'looking-for-feminist-sympathies-in-the-author' approach. It involves contextualizing the cultural production of the plays in an historical understanding of the complexities of Elizabethan society and the position of women. Although there is no absolute agreement on what this position was exactly, it is at least agreed that it was complex, a view which has now overturned Dusinberre's simplistic claim for the advancement of women. The opening scene to *King Lear*, for instance, traditionally read and played as Lear's misreading of Cordelia's filial affections, could be re-read and staged in terms of Elizabethan views on kingship, the organization of the family/household, marriage contracts, and the private/public positions of women. (See also Jardine 1989 [1983]; Belsey 1991 [1985], and discussion of these in Chapter 3 pp. 37–8.)

In the course of her analysis of Shakespeare, Mcluskie stresses the need to consider the practical as well as the textual aspects of the drama, but consideration of the plays as theatre has often been left out of the feminist frame. Even feminist studies of Shakespeare which have intersected with 'new' critical positions and methodologies have insisted on introducing the plays as 'literary texts' (see Lenz, Greene, and Neely 1980: 8). Feminist consideration of the staging of Shakespeare involves giving attention to the all-male theatrical context. Exceptionally, feminist critics who have addressed this context, like Lisa Jardine (1989), have had to face up to the difficulty of analysing what audiences 'saw' when Rosalind in *As You Like It*, for example, played by a boy, disguised herself as a boy, and then pretended to play the part of a woman in a mock-wooing scene, opposite her lover, Orlando, played also by a male performer. Homoerotic readings of such scenes are persuasively argued for by Case (1988: 22–3), though it is at this juncture that the theorization of what was 'seen' is at its most speculative. As Lorraine Helms argues: 'The convention of the boy actor vexes critical speculation. Cross-casting marks the nexus of character and performer in subtle and shifting ways which historical inquiry cannot recover' (1990: 197). It is impossible to know with certainty how the gender disguises were enacted on the Elizabethan stage, and what the spectator 'saw'. Yet although such speculation moves analysis into a 'grey' area, it at least acknowledges a complexity of gender based on an understanding of performance practice, as opposed to the feminist literary approach which, confined to the textual, makes claims for the positive representation of women but fails to consider what a so-called 'strong' female role might have looked like when played by a male performer. Case observes:

> These feminist critics do not deconstruct the powerful misogyny found in the image of a man playing Lady Macbeth and saying 'unsex me', nor do they account for the double

21

negative in *Twelfth Night*, in which two boys court one another, playing female characters.

(1988: 25)

In terms of modern performance of Shakespeare, there are those feminist practitioners who make a political decision not to perform in the 'classic' tradition, and women of a bourgeois-feminist persuasion who view performing Shakespeare as an opportunity to intervene in the contemporary production and reception of the plays. Helms articulates the extremes of choice for the performer as deciding between the view held by feminist critic Elaine Showalter that women playing the roles originally played by men will create 'new meanings and subversive tensions', and Case's suggestion that men should again play the roles as they were originally conceived as 'classic drag' (1990: 197–8). For the feminist practitioner who opts for performing Shakespeare, Helms offers a linguistic-based analysis (concentrating on the soliloquies) of where feminist intervention might take place. Carol Rutter (1988) interviews five commercially successful actresses who have all performed Shakespeare with the RSC: Sinead Cusack, Paola Dionisotti, Fiona Shaw, Juliet Stevenson, and Harriet Walter. Their joint introductory commentaries include trying to understand what it means to be playing women's roles as women, when they had originally been written to be played by boys, whilst admitting to the limitations imposed on them as actresses choosing to perform the 'classical repertoire' (xxiv–xxv). That said, in this context it is not Shakespeare the 'great feminist' who is invoked, but Shakespeare the 'great' role giver.

However, in the view of some feminist practitioners, playing 'radical' versions of Shakespeare's heroines in one of Britain's most theatrically prestigious venues is a contradiction in terms. The claims to be a 'radical' Lady Macbeth or Ophelia are militated against by the values encoded in Shakespeare as a cultural institution. Alan Sinfield, engaged in cultural-materialist analysis, explains the problematic ethos of 'Royal Shakespeare':

> The problem of course, is *Shakespeare* – the whole aura of elusive genius and institutionalised profundity. For even when the resistances set up by received notions of the plays are overcome and a genuinely radical interpretation is rendered persuasive (and it is not clear that this has oc- curred), the idea of the real Shakespeare from which it all

emanates nevertheless registers cultural authority, and implies that every innovation has been anticipated. The underlying pressure is towards deference and inertia.

(1985: 178)

However, Sinfield argues that the cultural and political authority of Shakespeare might be challenged if one were to 'take aspects of the plays and reconstitute them explicitly so that they become the vehicle of other values' (179). This is a route which other feminist practitioners have adopted in order to take issue with the canonical status accorded the Shakespeare repertoire. Like Wertenbaker's *The Love of the Nightingale* in the context of Greek theatre, *Lear's Daughters* by the Women's Theatre Group and Elaine Feinstein (1991), is one example of a materialist-feminist re-inscription of a Shakespearean 'classic'. *Lear's Daughters* foregrounds and re-tells the narratives of Goneril, Regan, and Cordelia. The stage action is controlled by the figure of an androgynous fool who functions as a mistress/master of ceremonies in the re-telling of the story, which demonstrates how three women are imprisoned in a patriarchal discourse which constructs them as three daughters. Feminist intervention succeeds in radically re-inscribing the patriarchal values of the Elizabethan text in a way which empowers the feminist spectator/reader to participate in changing them, rather than endorsing the value-system of the 'father' text.

THE 'LOST' FEMALE TRADITION

Examining the absence of women from the stage constitutes one branch of feminist theatre history. A further critical approach, working in tandem with the challenge to the 'canon', is the recovery of female-authored dramatic texts and theatrical contexts. In 1978, for example, the feminist theatre group Mrs Worthington's Daughters was formed with the specific aim of recovering 'lost' drama on or by women from the past (for details see Wandor 1986: 84). As a result of looking for and concentrating on women playwrights, feminist theatre scholarship has plotted a very different historico-theatrical map to that established by traditional canonical criticism. This section will briefly survey some of the examples of 'lost' female dramatists and practitioners.

Pioneering playwrights

Case (1988) in a chapter on 'Women Pioneers' charts the following 'firsts': Hrotsvit von Gandersheim was 'the first known woman playwright of written texts' (32); 'Aphra Behn was the first woman to make her living as a playwright' (36); 'Sor Juana was the first woman playwright in the New World to write plays that were performed and published' (41); Mrs Mercy Otis Warren was 'the first American woman playwright' (43). These are just a few of the examples of women dramatists whose work has been 'hidden' from view. This section overviews three examples of playwrighting by women which have recently been recovered by feminist scholarship. Chapter 8, a case study of the American dramatist Susan Glaspell, complements this overview, and demonstrates in more detail how the bias of the canon works to conceal women's drama.

Hrotsvit

Arguing the case for the reinstatement of Hrotsvit as an important 'first' in women's theatre has been considerable. The argument comes in two parts: first, why Hrotsvit was left out of the canon when her 'catalog of pioneering achievements', not least of which is the claim that 'her dramas are the first performable plays of the Middle Ages', is outstanding (Wilson 1984: 30); and second, why a reassessment of her work is seen by feminist scholars as an essential exercise.

The answer to the first point lies, as it repeatedly does in the case of 'lost' women writers, in the bias of the canon and the critical scholarship which surrounds it. Sigrid Novak, writing on the invisibility of Hrotsvit and other female playwrights in the canon of German theatre, attributed her invisibility to the 'prejudice that women are incapable of good dramatic production' and the 'underrating of plays because professional critics – traditionally men – have used male psychology as the criterion for judging female characters in plays by women' (1972: 47). Sister Mary Marguerite Butler's full-length study put forward the case for the 'stageworthiness' of Hrotsvit's theatre, and exhumed the plays from a literary tradition of male scholarship by working through a 'critical theatre approach to the plays' (1960: 19). As more about the dramatic traditions of Hrotsvit's work came to light, so too did the critical prejudice surrounding it.

The pattern of an historical 'silencing' of women's texts appears to occur whenever and wherever female authorship critiques or ridicules the forms and ideologies of dominant culture. The heroines in Hrotsvit's theatre, for example, work against the Terentian dramatic tradition which depicted women as 'lascivious and shameless' (Wilson 1984: 38). Hrotsvit generically undermines a model of comedy based on the debasement and objectification of women by men. This is exemplified in her second play *Dulcitius*, when the holy virgins Agapes, Chionia, and Hirena are imprisoned and are under threat of rape from the governer Dulcitius. When he comes to 'satisfy' himself 'in their longed-for embrace' (Hrotsvit 1984: 55), the prayers of the virgins are answered as the would-be rapist is deluded into sublimating his desires with kitchen pots and pans: 'The women watch Dulcitius and giggle. In their laughter and his foolishness as a result of their spell-binding power, the women dominate the rapist. The male dramatic perspective has been reversed' (Case 1983: 537).

Second, the importance of reclaiming Hrotsvit lies in the way in which discovering the 'past' is a means to changing the future. If the patriarchal canon of literary and theatrical 'greats' is to be centrally deconstructed, then women's work from the past has to come out of the margins of oblivion in order to secure a future for the creative work of women in theatre. Case observes:

> the canon reproduces its history in its future. Without a primary position in the canon for Hrotsvit in the role of the first woman playwright, women's plays will remain invisible, minor, or at best 'separate but equal' – ghettoized in women's anthologies, women's performance groups and women's studies.
>
> (1983: 535)

Without primary role models, such as Hrotsvit, it may not be possible to establish a tradition of women's dramatic writing as a 'norm' rather than as an 'alternative' or deviant off-shoot of the 'canon' which perpetuates the dramatic forms and ideological concerns of the dominant (male) culture.

That said, the concept of a 'canon' of women's theatre risks the danger of subscribing to the values of the male canon. June Schlueter, who has edited two volumes on the American canon, one devoted to feminist re-readings of the male canon (1989), the second concerned with the female canon (1990), raises this point:

'the danger is that in operating out of self-interest, no matter how rightly conceived, female academicians may create an alternative "canon" no more balanced or representative than the one we have inherited' (1990: 13). Schlueter's observation is addressed and exemplified in the final contribution to the volume by Hart – 'Canonizing Lesbians?' – which interrogates the position of lesbian theatre in relation to the 'canon', and in doing so challenges not only the concept of the 'canonical' but also the assumptions made in labelling it 'female' (1990: 275–92).

Aphra Behn and Restoration 'female wits'

Despite these dangers and difficulties, finding a female tradition has been important to a feminist history of the theatre which has felt the need to discover its female 'firsts'. The feminist recovery of Aphra Behn was important in this respect because of the role model she represented to contemporary literary women. Her biographer, the playwright Maureen Duffy, seeking to undo the 'fictionalizing process' which 'has taken over to make nonsense or romance of the facts of her life', claims Behn as 'the first woman in England to earn her living as a professional writer' (1977: 23). Behn, the professional writer, was subsequently claimed by feminist theatre historians as Behn the 'hard-driving professional playwright, independent, bawdy, witty, and tough' (Cotton 1980: 55).

More importantly, some American and British feminist theatre historians looked beyond the recovery of one 'great' female playwright to excavating the 'lost' work of several women playwrights from the Restoration period (see Cotton 1980; Morgan 1981). In concluding the introduction to her collection of Restoration plays by women, Fidelis Morgan notes:

in all of London's theatres during the sixty years from 1920 to 1980 (a time which boasts huge social and political advances for women) fewer plays by women writers have been performed than were played by the two London companies which held the dramatic monopoly from 1660 to 1720.

(1981: xi)

Morgan and Lyons (1991) argue that the plays in this second Restoration collection (by Aphra Behn, the mysterious 'Ariadne', Mary Pix, and Centlivre) 'were every bit as successful as those by male playwrights of their times' (vi). Morgan and Lyons, however, demonstrate how it is that a dramatist like Aphra Behn, whose work was popular for a further fifty years after her death, is written out of the canon. They describe the changing attitudes towards women, the growth of the 'cult of "femininity"' in the eighteenth and nineteenth centuries. In short, 'the requirement that a female writer be conspicuously "feminine" was ultimately to cut Aphra Behn out of English Literature' (1991: xv).

Like Hrotsvit, Behn has now been the subject of several major studies and conferences (see Trussler's 'further reading' on Behn, 1986: 16). Ironically her rediscovery in Britain was most publicly confirmed by the RSC's 'star' or 'classic' production of her play *The Rover* (1986), with Jeremy Irons in the title role. Working against the 'classic' tradition of performance is Morgan's own performance-lecture *The Female Wits* which she tours nationally with three other actresses. Its combines the information-giving technique of a 'reading' with performed extracts of plays by Behn and her contemporaries, as a means of performing a feminist criticism of the 'canon', and informing the spectator of this 'lost' tradition of women's playwrighting.

Suffrage playwrights

In terms of recovering traditions of female playwrighting, the period of suffrage drama in the context of British theatre history has been the subject of substantial recent feminist scholarship. This interest was fuelled by the parallels that could be drawn between the political and theatrical activity of the suffrage years at the turn of the century, and the Women's Liberation Movement of the 1970s. The recovery of late nineteenth-century women playwrights has radically altered the canon of 'new drama'. Traditional, literary-orientated studies of the 'new drama' tend to focus on an all-male cast of playwrights. Jan McDonald (1986), for example, surveys Barker, Glasworthy, Hankin, and Masefield. In overviews of the period from a more theatrical base suffrage drama is rarely mentioned (for an example, see Trewin 1976). However, feminist intervention in this period of British theatre has recovered a number of women playwrights who contributed in mainstream and 'alternative' theatre contexts to the Edwardian debate on suffrage and the Woman Question. The historico-theatrical map can now be re-charted to include women play-wrights such as Elizabeth Baker (1876–1962), Elizabeth Robins

(1862–1952), Cicely Hamilton (1872–1952), and Githa Sowerby (1876–1970). (See Fitzsimmons and Gardner 1991 for a selection of plays by these writers; Stowell 1992a for a full-length study of women's dramatic authorship of the period; Gardner 1985, and Spender and Hayman 1985 for collections of suffrage plays, sketches, and monologues.)

The parallels between the First and Second Women's Liberation Movement have, however, tended to obscure other 'stages' of women's theatre this century, indicative of the danger that feminist theatre scholarship may itself distort the recovery of women's drama and theatre. This arises, for example, if historical stages are measured by a 'post-liberation' concept of feminism. Michelene Wandor's overview of women and theatre in the twentieth century dwells on the suffrage theatre at the turn of the century, glosses the 1920s and 1930s as a period when 'organised political feminism was far less visible', and moves on to the period after the Second World War when 'feminism and theatre again came together' (1986: 3). Wandor admits that the 1920s and 1930s was a period when 'struggles to improve the position of women in society continued, but less publicly' (ibid.), but evaluating the inter-war period as unworthy of interest because it did not give a public face to feminism means that the significant number of women writing and working in theatre during this period are overlooked and 'lost' to view. (Some of this work has now been recovered: see Gale 1988.)

'Lost' practitioners

Although this feminist re-charting of an historical canon of plays by women constitutes a useful and necessary part of challenging the male bias of the 'canon', it does not engage in a more radical re-thinking of what constitutes theatre history. Susan Bassnett has argued that feminist theatre history needs to ask more questions about the *context* in which women's work is produced:

> We need to stop thinking about the 'exceptions' such as Hrostvitha or Aphra Behn, and look seriously at the contexts in which those women were writing and the tradition out of which they wrote, accepting that the small list of names we have could be very much longer.
>
> (1989b: 112)

Bassnett is critical of 'the emphasis of so much theatre scholarship on text-based theatre' which 'creates an imbalance' (108). To illustrate her point she cites the pre-Renaissance performance conditions when 'the actor performing a scenario or play was one of a much wider group of dancers, singers, musicians, jugglers and artistes of all kinds' (ibid.). Although the emphasis on the dramatic text has hindered investigation into theatrical texts and contexts, feminist theatre history has begun to move in this direction in the following key areas: actresses and their working conditions; women as theatrical managers and directors; and the female performer as text.

Actresses and their working conditions

The mythology of the actress as prostitute, popularized throughout different periods of theatre history, has been deconstructed by feminist approaches to theatre history which detail the working conditions of the female performer. This is exemplified in two recent full-length studies by Elizabeth Howe (1992) and Tracy Davis (1991) which respectively document the working conditions of the actress in the Restoration and Victorian periods. Howe's study of the first English actresses points to the gender-based inequalities of the profession which employed men in far greater numbers than women, did not allow women to become a 'sharer' in either of the two companies formed after 1660, and, with the exception of a few female 'stars', paid women lower wages than men (1992: 26–7). Furthermore, the dramatic/theatrical representation of women as sexually available, coupled with the sexual harassment of women off-stage, suggests that 'society in general seems to have considered the actress fair game' (33). In the case of the star actress Elizabeth Barry, Howe observes that the contemporary image of this actress as 'mercenary prostitute', given that there was 'scant evidence that she actually *was* a prostitute', reflects a 'misogynist resentment of a woman who achieved popularity, power, and, above all, material success in a public career' (30). Howe estimates that only about a quarter of the actresses on the Restoration stage that we know about were considered by their contemporaries to lead respectable lives (33).

Davis's investigation into the working lives of the actresses on the Victorian stage details a similar picture of economic hardship: 'women's sufferings were particularly acute, for their basic rates of pay were lower, their professional expenses were higher, and their competition for employment grew more intense in the latter decades of the century'(1991: 35). But, just as Howe demonstrates in the context of the seventeenth-century stage, it is the prevailing attitude towards women in nineteenth-century society in general, and towards the actress in particular, which, Davis argues, constitutes the reality behind the myth of the actress as prostitute:

> Society's ideology about women and prescriptions of female sexuality were constantly defied by the actress whose independence, education, allure, and flouting of sexual mores (unavoidable conditions of the work) gave her access to the male ruling elite while preventing her from being accepted by right-thinking and – especially – feminine society.
>
> (Davis 1991: 69–70; see also Kent 1980)

Women as theatrical managers and directors

One of the ways in which the exceptional star actress might increase her power within the profession was by moving into theatrical management. It was the norm for successful actors to have a share in company profits in the seventeenth and eighteenth centuries (see Howe 1992: 8), or to run their own companies as actor–managers in the nineteenth century, but there were also a few, exceptional women who traded their financial success as performers for managerial status. The recovery of such women has been viewed as significant, not only because it is important to know that there were women who achieved 'male' managerial status, but also to analyse what changes and improvements might be made to the artistic programmes and the working conditions of a theatre when a woman was in charge.

In terms of Edwardian theatre, for example, when women were able to take on managerial positions of authority, they frequently demonstrated an interest in nurturing new writing and new styles of theatrical practice. In turn, this meant that new women dramatists might compete equally with male writers to have their plays put on, and not be subjected to the usual misogynist views on women playwrights which forced them into writing under male pseudonyms. Actress–manager Lena Ashwell, who managed the Kingsway Theatre and was committed to the encouragement of new writing, read and selected Diana of Dobson's by Cicely

Hamilton (see Stowell 1992b: 179). Annie Horniman, who was the financial backer and manager of Manchester's Gaiety Theatre at the turn of the century, had a reputation for fair play when it came to reading scripts (see Holledge 1981: 41). She encouraged a modern repertoire of plays by new, young writers of both sexes, and a style of performance which required a levelling of status in the interests of creating an ensemble company with equal opportunities for men and women (see Aston 1992a: 206). Even the star actress Sarah Bernhardt, whose international standing was built on a series of popular histrionic vehicles, showed that in her capacity as a theatrical manager she was also interested in and prepared to risk staging (at considerable financial loss), work by unknown, young playwrights (see Stokes in Stokes, Booth and Bassnett 1988: 24).

Moreover, it is in this period of theatre history that the role of the director emerges in experimental forms of theatre, but modern surveys of the 'birth of the director' (see Braun 1982) make no mention of any women working in this capacity or of the 'alternative' experimental women's theatre groups. André Antoine's Paris-based Théâtre Libre is widely acknowledged as the prototype for an alternative, ensemble-styled company, though the Théâtre féministe founded by Marya-Chéliga in 1897 to encourage the work of female playwrights is never mentioned as a native descendant of this style of theatrical practice (see Aston 1986). Similarly, the work of the Independent Theatre and the Stage Society has been well documented (see Woodfield 1984), but the work of Edy Craig and her company of Pioneer Players, organized along similar lines to the 'new', experimental groups, but with one notable difference: ' all the areas of the company's work were dominated by women', has not (Holledge 1981: 123). Christine Dymkowski identifies the ways in which Craig's work as a director and the company's style of theatrical practice has been obscured in the first instance by the attitude of a significant number of contemporary male, mainstream critics, and subsequently by male theatre historians (1992: 230). Yet the work of this company is important to feminist theatre history because it offers a primary model for women's theatrical group practice. As Dymkowski describes:

> Women carried out the production work, while Edy Craig designed many of the sets and directed most of the sixty-five plays produced in the thirty-seven subscription programmes.

The plays the society performed showed a similar commitment: not only did they provide a large number of parts for women, but many were also written by women.

(1992: 222)

This suggests that Case's argument for the reinstatement of Hrotsvit in the dramatic canon has a parallel in the production context. The role models of women directors, managers, companies, etc., are also a necessary and vital part of establishing a 'history' of feminist performance.

Female performer as text

Feminist intervention in understanding theatre as a sign-system has also opened up the possibilities of analysing the female performer as the author of a potentially subversive theatrical site/ sight in mainstream historical stages. Historical reconstruction of the body as sign-system is inevitably limited and speculative, particularly as such reconstructions are dependent on sources such as (male) reviewing. That said, it does propose a feminist line of enquiry whose premise is founded on the notion of theatre as multi-authored, rather than adhering to the conservative principle, as so much of text-bound feminist criticism does, of the single (male) author/dramatist as the controlling agent of theatrical production. The female performer as potential creator of an 'alternative' text to the male-authored stage picture in which she is 'framed', is then made available for consideration. Those sign-systems which make up the 'alternative' text and might be historically reconstructed include: the signs which are generated by the physical attributes of the performer (facial features, height, body size, colouring, hair, ethnicity, etc.); the artifice of self-presentation according to codes of theatrical convention (e.g. costuming, make-up, etc.); the 'star' signs, whether professional (association with a type of role, style of performance, theatrical management, etc.) or personal (association with a particular lifestyle, lover, political cause, etc.); the gestural signs (style and systems of facial and body movements, etc.; the vocal signs (vocal range, techniques and conventions of delivery, patterns of intonation, etc.).

The work of several of the nineteenth-century star actresses has been re-evaluated in ways which have had recourse to this kind of methodology. One of the key reasons for this is that the 'star' actress of the last century, who performed internationally and therefore to audiences speaking many different languages, needed to create her own 'text' to make her theatre understood. In his essay on the Polish star Helena Modjeska, John Stokes, for instance, comments as follows:

> This allowed a further kind of language, a theatrical 'body-language', which like any other language, nevertheless allowed development, variation, refinement much depending upon the ways in which individual actresses could extemporise, as it were, with their own bodies and their facial exressions upon established codes.
>
> (1992: 19)

In the introduction to the full-length study of the three international stars Bernhardt, Terry, and Duse, Stokes, Booth and Bassnett acknowledge the difficulty of reconstructing the performances, especially when 'all three actresses have passed into mythology and have created their own sign-system of legend' (1988: 10). However, they argue for a methodology of research which will recover the 'visual' dimension of the stage pictures containing these performers, looking to 'set and costume designs, promptbooks and rehearsal copies' to understand 'the spatial patterns they imply', in order that 'at the points of intersection, we can discover the visible presence of the performance that really signified' (6). (For further examples, see Aston 1989 on Bernhardt; Aston 1992b on Ristori; Clarke 1992 on Patrick Campbell.)

This kind of historical recovery has meant that traditions of theatre which have had a 'visual' emphasis, like the nineteenth-century stage, and were excluded from the literary scholarship of theatre history because of this, are reclaimed in a way which unfixes male-defined boundaries of 'high' and 'low' culture. The unfixing of 'status' boundaries has been important to feminist criticism because it has generally meant the recovery of women's cultural forms which have been labelled as 'low-status' in canonical terms, and therefore 'lost' to view. One female performance tradition which has been recovered as a result of the unfixing of cultural 'status', for example, is the stage history of women cross-dressing: a history of female performers whose text is the alienation of the 'body-as-text'. Study of the English stage of the 1660s has been important to feminist scholarship, not just because women were deemed to make their 'first' appearance on the

English stage, but because actresses no sooner entered/re-entered the theatre than they began to take on breeches (male) roles (see Wandor 1986: Chapter 2). Neither was this early cross-dressing by women an isolated phenomenon. Travesti appearances have been documented throughout the eighteenth and nineteenth centuries, and have been most significantly reclaimed from outside the margins of 'legitimate', 'high-status' theatre, specifically the British music-hall of the last century (see Maitland 1986; Aston 1988; Bratton 1992). The attraction lies in the subversive potential of the male impersonator, the 'most highly-charged and disturbing of theatrical devices', to 'cross' the gender divide (Senelick 1982: 40). The critical practice of feminist theatre history which has critiqued the acting tradition of the Western 'classic' stage, where the representation of women is controlled by men, explains the attraction for the feminist critic of finding a tradition in which it is the female performer who constructs the male as sign.

Whether deconstructing the canon or recovering a tradition of women's theatre and theatrical practice, feminist theatre history no longer accepts the concept of a theatrical tradition which either excludes women or considers them 'lost'. In the early 1980s Britain's longest running feminist theatre company, the Women's Theatre Group, toured a number of plays which dramatized a feminist re-visioning of male versions of history. In their devised play *Time Pieces*, which re-charts women's twentieth-century history, they called on their female audiences to:

> . . . move with the pictures you see on the screen
> And seek out the women whose stories have been
> Ever shrouded and hidden from popular view.
> They could be related to any one of you.
> (Wakefield and the Women's Theatre Group 1984: 128)

By analogy, bringing the 'lost' tradition of women's theatre history into view is an important political step if feminist theatre scholarship is to change the future history of the stage.

3

FEMINIST THEORIES OF REPRESENTATION
The case against realism

Feminist scholarship in recent years has been centrally concerned with the theoretical discourses of representation articulated
through the texts of a number of cultural fields: art, cinema, media,
advertising, theatre, etc. In consequence, feminist analysis of
representation has identified the oppressive discourse of engendered representation which constructs and positions 'woman'
as 'the other-from-man' (De Lauretis 1984: 5). This chapter aims
to survey some of the key areas of feminist study where critical
intervention in the fictional construct of 'woman' has been taken
up in feminist approaches to the study of theatre, beginning with
a brief overview of feminism and Lacanian psychoanalysis, the
theoretical apparatus which underpins work on the construction
of the feminine subject. (The reader who is unfamiliar with this
field may find it useful to refer to the two introductory chapters
in Mitchell and Rose (1982), which were used to shape the
contextualizing section of this chapter; see below.)

FEMINISM AND LACAN

Understanding how the feminine subject is constructed, examining
feminine sexuality, 'goes beyond psychoanalysis to feminism, as
part of its questioning of how that sexuality comes to be defined'
(Rose, in Mitchell and Rose 1982: 27). Furthermore, Jacqueline Rose
explains, 'psychoanalysis is now recognised as crucial in the
discussion of femininity – how it comes into being and what it
might mean' and identifies the centrality of Jacques Lacan to 'the
controversies produced by that recognition' (ibid.). Lacan, director
of the *école freudienne* in Paris from 1964 until 1980, proposed a re-
framing of Freud, a 'reorienting' of 'psychoanalysis to its task of

deciphering the ways in which the human subject is constructed' which has since been taken up by feminism in order to critique the construction of the 'feminine' (Mitchell and Rose 1982: 5).

What Lacan had at his disposal, which Freud did not, was the science of linguistics pioneered in the twentieth century by Saussure. Lacan claimed that subjectivity is constructed through the linguistic sign-system of language. In the Lacanian system the point at which a child enters language is metaphorically represented as the 'mirror stage' (see Rose in Mitchell and Rose 1982: 30–1). The entry into language constitutes the entry into an external order which constructs the child's identity. In psychosexual terms it is also the moment when the child's pre-Oedipal link with the mother is severed: a splitting which requires the repression of the desire for the mother which is experienced as a loss or lack. The pre-Oedipal phase is termed the Imaginary. The entry into language is posited as an entry into an order which represents the Law of the Father (and the loss of the mother) and is therefore classed as the Symbolic Order. Feminism and psychoanalysis in a post-Lacanian context has been principally concerned with exposing how the arbitrarily imposed Symbolic (phallic) Order in which all subjects as members of a communicating social order are required to participate, privileges the male at the expense of the female. Post-Lacanian psychoanalytical approaches have been used to 'read' different types of cultural texts and contexts.

Cultural-materialist Catherine Belsey has considered the Lacanian notion of the split 'I' in literary contexts (1980). The entry into language, Belsey explains, splits the subject into 'the subject of the enunciation and the subject of the *énoncé*, the "I" who speaks and the "I" who is represented in the discourse' (85). She then considers this 'contradiction in the subject' in relation to texts which she identifies as 'classic realist' (85) and those which she classifies as 'interrogative' (91). Those literary texts which belong to Belsey's definition of 'classic realism' are symbolic: offer a stable subject positioning, fix meaning, move towards closure, etc. Texts which operate in the mode of classic realism seek to repress the split in the subject: to anaesthetize the desire for the Imaginary. Those which are defined as 'interrogative' demonstrate an 'unfixing' of the subject, a destabilizing of meaning, and acknowledge the painful suturing of the Imaginary and the Symbolic. Belsey argues that in the classic realist text the contradiction in the subject is suppressed in 'the interests of the stability of a class society'. By contrast, it is the instability of the subject which characterizes the interrogative text which appears 'at times of crisis in the social formation' and is indicative of a desire for change (85–6).

In the Lacanian model the position of the female subject is, however, one of double alienation. As Case explains:

> If I might expand Lacan's metaphor in order to include the possibility of the female subject, 'she' also sees in that mirror that she is a woman. At that moment she further fractures, split once as the male-identified subject and his subjectivity and split once more as the woman who observes her own subject position as both male-identified and female.
>
> (1989a: 130–1)

As Case continues, the female subject 'cannot appear as a single, whole, continuous subject as the male can because she senses that his story is not her story', and therefore enters 'the doors of discourse in male drag' (131). Or, put another way, the female subject is silenced.

The historical evolution of the silencing of women is extensively explored in Belsey's full-length study of Renaissance drama (1991 [1985]) which offers a cultural-materialist analysis of subjectivity in the sixteenth and seventeenth centuries. The study critiques the historical construction of the subject from the erosion of absolutism to an emergent liberal humanism through an examination of dramatic, fictional, and non-fictional texts. The ordering of material into two parts: 'Part One: Man', 'Part Two: Woman' is indicative of the engendering of the subject position which Belsey charts. The invitation of liberal humanism to construct the subject as a unified entity cannot be the same for women as it is for men:

> The subject of liberal humanism claims to be the unified, autonomous author of his or her own choices (moral, electoral and consumer), and the source and origin of speech. Women in Britain for most of the sixteenth and seventeenth centuries were not fully any of these things. Able to speak, to take up a subject-position in discourse, to identify with the 'I' of utterance and the uttering 'I' which always exceeds it, they were none the less enjoined to silence, discouraged from any form of speech which was not an act of submission to the authority of their fathers or husbands.
>
> (149)

37

Feminist Renaissance scholar Lisa Jardine offers similar observations on the silencing of women in the Renaissance period (1989 [1983]). Jardine, like Belsey, consults a number of Renaissance dramas and other types of text from the period in order to demonstrate the 'case for silence as the domestic ideal in women' (106). Women's gossiping and scolding, on the other hand, were seen as disruptive and as a threat to the patriarchal (symbolic) order (107).

At the close of her Renaissance study, Belsey proposes that women's alienation as subjects in relation to the Symbolic Order creates an 'absence which a feminism that refuses the liberal-humanist modes of self-fulfilment is able to appropriate for politics'. To 'problematize the liberal-humanist alliance with patriarchy, to formulate a sexual politics', is 'to begin the struggle for change' (1991: 221). In contemporary feminist theatre where women have been seeking to take up a subject position they have looked to the 'interrogative' style of text and performance practice, in which the contradiction of the subject is split open in the interests of challenging and changing the symbolic or social orders. What women have contested and resisted are the oppressive systems of symbolic closure which, for example, characterize the dominant theatrical traditions of staging realism.

FEMINISM, REALISM, AND NARRATIVES OF DESIRE

The oppressive systems of symbolic closure which characterize classic realism are further critiqued by feminist critical theory concerned with subject positioning and narrative. Early formalist and structuralist approaches to textual study encompassed the possibility of establishing a universal model of narrative. Key studies by, amongst others, Propp, Barthes, and Greimas, proposed and debated the possibilities of an underlying structural grammar of narrative, central to which was the concept of a 'quest'-based model. Subsequent feminist intervention in the field of narrative, however, has demonstrated the 'object' positioning of the female subject in such a model. In the context of feminist film studies, Teresa De Lauretis offered an approach to narrative which has influenced many feminists working on narrative and representation in different areas of cultural production, including theatre.

38

De Lauretis engages with the formalist and structuralist approaches to show how narrative strategies are engendered: how the 'male' initiates the quest, but the 'female' can only be the object of that quest (1984: Chapter 5). For example, she analyses Propp's seven 'spheres of action' which constitute the narrative model for the folktale (Propp 1968 [1928]). In this model, the fourth 'sphere of action' is that of a *princess* (a sought-for person) and of *her father*' (Propp 1968: 79). Propp qualifies this as follows:

> the princess and her father cannot be exactly delineated from each other according to functions. Most often it is the father who assigns difficult tasks due to the hostile feeling toward the suitor. He also frequently punishes (or orders punished) the false hero.
>
> (79–80)

De Lauretis explicates this 'sphere of action' as one which positions the female as a site of transaction between the old generation of patriarchy (father) and the new (lover/husband-to-be). The female is therefore inactive, is defined only in terms of the male (as daughter, as wife-to-be), is, in short, the object of the male/hero's quest, but not a subject or initiator of action in her own right. De Lauretis applies her critique to readings of the narrative strategies of mainstream cinematic forms.

The feminist analysis of Propp, *à la* De Lauretis, could similarly be applied to the actantial model of Greimas which proposes a schema based on six functions (Sender, Subject, Object, Helper, Opponent, Receiver), and which has had a wider application in dramatic and theatrical contexts (for an accessible introduction to Greimas in a theatre context see Aston and Savona 1991: 37–42). To give an example of an actantial model: in a traditional love narrative the hero (Subject), under the influence of love (Sender), seeks the heroine (Object), as a result of his own desire (Receiver), and is aided by friends (Helper/s), or opposed by his adversaries, often the heroine's father/guardian (Opponent/s). In a critique of Greimas, based on the idea of a linguistic re-framing of the actantial model, Barthes proposes (although does not pursue) the notion that the model offers 'a privileged class of actors . . . (the subject of the quest, of the desire, of the action)' (1977 [1966]: 109). Feminist methodology, along the lines proposed by De Lauretis, might develop this by demonstrating the gender bias of the model: the 'privileged class of actors' is male (signified in the use of the term 'actor' to designate performer). The 'quest', the 'desire', the 'action' are all male-determined and male-centred, and are privileged at the expense of the female.

De Lauretis pursues her analysis by examining the Soviet semiotician Jurij Lotman's essay on plot typology (1979), which proposes a narrative model consisting of 'a simple chain of two functions, open at both ends and thus endlessly repeatable: "entry into a closed space, and emergence from it"' (De Lauretis 1984: 118). Moreover, in terms of Lotman's 'mythical-textual mechanics' structuration is implicitly based on sexual difference, given that it requires that the hero (male, 'regardless of the gender of the text-image') negotiate the 'obstacle' which 'whatever its personification, is morphologically female and indeed, simply, the womb' (118–19). In short:

> The hero, the mythical subject, is constructed as human being and as male; he is the active principle of culture, the establisher of distinction, the creator of differences. Female is what is not susceptible to transformation, to life or death; she (it) is an element of plot-space, a topos, a resistance, matrix and matter.
>
> (119)

Feminist critical approaches to theatre have made use of this work to analyse subject positioning and narrative in dramatic and theatrical contexts. In particular it has been used to further a feminist critique of realism. In narrative terms, dramatic and theatrical texts in the realist tradition operate systems of 'closure'. Their well-constructed or well-made forms follow a linear pattern from exposition to crisis and ultimate resolution. The subject of this narrative is male and its discourse is phallocentric: is expressive of male experience, emotions, etc. By contrast, the 'female' is enclosed within the male narratives of realism, is most commonly defined in relation to the male 'subject' (as wife, mother, daughter, etc.), is unable to take up a subject position (as previously described), and is used as an object of exchange in an heterosexual, male economy.

The narrative strategies of 'realism' and its bourgeois ideologies have been critiqued by both feminist theatre scholars and practitioners. Case has argued that 'the heterosexist ideology linked with its stage partner, realism, is directed against women ... the closure of these realistic narratives chokes the women to death and strangles the play of symbols, the possibility of seduction' (1989b: 297). 'Cast the realism aside – its consequences for women are deadly' she concludes (ibid.). Playwright Caryl Churchill has echoed this view: 'I remember . . . thinking of the "maleness" of the traditional structure of plays, with conflict and building in a certain way to a climax' (quoted in Fitzsimmons 1989: 90).

Feminist case studies of canonical 'greats' in the realist tradition which investigate 'male' narrative structures, bear out the impression of what Churchill describes as the 'maleness' of conventional dramatic forms. For example, Schlueter's collection of essays on male-authored American drama (1989) offers four feminist re-readings of Arthur Miller. The first of these, by Gayle Austin, is, of the four, the most cogent and incisively argued re-reading of narrative and gender issues. Austin explains her choice of text by alluding to the reputation of *Death of a Salesman* (1949) as 'the "Daddy" of American drama and a frequently utilized paradigm for what American drama *is* or should be'(1989: 59). Austin adapts the anthropological approach proposed by Gayle Rubin in her influential essay 'The Traffic in Women' (1975) which identifies the '"exchange of women"' within 'social systems' as a site of oppression (Rubin 1975: 175). By using Rubin's approach (a complex meshing of Marx, Freud, and Lévi-Strauss), Austin demonstrates the narrative structures of the play which deny women the possibility of taking up an 'active' subject position. In such a reading Linda Loman can only be inscribed in her husband's 'story'; is, in De Lauretis's terms, a 'place' her husband passes through to his tragic destination. (Austin's essay moves on to contrast Miller's 'classic' with Lillian Hellman's *Another Part of the Forest* (1946), which Austin argues does position women differently: as 'active subjects', 'making efforts to arrange their own exchange among men' (63).)

THE GAZE

In her work on narrative, De Lauretis compares Lotman's 'pattern of mythical narrative' to the discussion of narrative and sadism by feminist film critic Laura Mulvey in her seminal essay 'Visual Pleasure and Narrative Cinema' (1975). Mulvey's observations on sadism, narrative, and the female subject are part of her critique of 'the male gaze' in mainstream film texts:

In a world ordered by sexual imbalance, pleasure in looking has been split between active/male and passive/female. The determining male gaze projects its phantasy on to the female figure which is styled accordingly. In their traditional exhibitionist role women are simultaneously looked at and displayed, with their appearance coded for strong visual and erotic impact so that they can be said to connote *to-be-looked-at-ness*.

(1975: 11)

Feminists, working through psychosemiotics, have critiqued the gaze in several major full-length film studies which, in addition to the work of Mulvey and De Lauretis, include Kaplan (1983), Silverman (1983), and Doane (1987).

Outside of the feminist film studies context the construction of Woman as object-to-be-looked-at has been critiqued in a number of dominant 'high' and 'low' cultural forms which represent women on display. Berger (1972), for example, identified female objectification in the 'high' cultural context of European oil painting, which reproduced the unequal power relations of a society in which *'men act* and *women appear'* (47). Pornography's representation of women for male consumption has been a key target of feminism. As Coward argues: 'the female body is the place where this society writes its sexual messages. Nowhere is this more so than in pornography – a series of images which are used almost exclusively by men' (1984: 60; for further discussion on pornography see Chapter 9, pp. 128–32). However, Coward goes on to identify the ways in which the images of women produced for male consumption in pornography are also more widely encoded in other legitimate media such as fashion photography. In an earlier essay she states:

the direct look of the woman to the viewer, who identifies with the position of the camera, for example, pervades not only fashion magazines and advertising images but is also characteristic of 'portrait' photography and is emulated in the upmarket snapshot. Certain postures – again dominant in pornography – appear indissolubly linked in the ideologies of 'good photography' with representations of women.

(Coward 1982: 16)

The problem for the woman-as-viewer, the female spectator, is how can she 'look' when the economy of the gaze is male? The problem may be briefly illustrated by providing an example from a theatre context: *Death of a Salesman*.

Death of a Salesman: the 'gaze' of classic realism

Miller's *Death of a Salesman*, as previously stated, is emblematic of the oppressive systems of closure which the dominant tradition of staging classic realism presents for the female subject. The 'I' of the dramatic discourse is male, and the female subject, to paraphrase Case, is in 'male drag'. Actantially she is positioned in the agent of Linda Loman as the 'helper' (handmaiden) in the ejaculatory narrative of the American Dream, which is not her narrative. Ideologically, she is an object of exchange in a heterosexual economy founded on bourgeois familial relations.

There comes a moment in the play when, in cameo, Miller stages the construction of the gaze. This occurs in Act One in a split-scene staging in which the salesman, Willy Loman, is seen in the present with his wife, and in the past with his mistress:

> (*Music is heard as behind a scrim, to the left of the house, the* WOMAN, *dimly seen, is dressing.*)
>
> WILLY (*with great feeling*): You're the best there is, Linda, you're a pal, you know that? On the road – on the road I want to grab you sometimes and just kiss the life outa you.
>
> (*The laughter is loud now, and he moves into a brightening area at the left, where the* WOMAN *has come from behind the scrim and is standing, putting on her hat, looking into a 'mirror', and laughing.*)
>
> WILLY: 'Cause I get so lonely – especially when business is bad and there's nobody to talk to. I get the feeling that I'll never sell anything again, that I won't make a living for you, or a business, a business for the boys. (*He talks through the* WOMAN's *subsiding laughter; the* WOMAN *primps at the 'mirror'.*)
>
> (Miller 1961 [1949]: 29)

Miller's construction of universal 'Woman', looking into the mirror, emblematizes the 'to-be-looked-at-ness' of the male gaze. If the female spectator identifies with the 'Woman', then she reproduces herself as an object of desire for male consumption. If she identifies with the wife she agrees to her subordinate position

43

within the heterosexual economy and the sadistic narrative frame which denies her access to her own story. The alienated position of the female spectator is reinforced by (male) dramatic criticism of the play, which assumes she will identify with the 'hero'. 'Death of a Salesman is a play written along the lines of the finest classical tragedy. It is the revelation of a man's downfall, a destruction whose roots are entirely in his own soul', writes one reviewer. Another states of the play that 'there is such truth in it that it is hard to see how any sensitive playgoer of mature years can fail to find something of himself in the mirror it holds up to life' (quoted in Bigsby 1987: 24–5; the emphases are mine). These commentaries assume that the female spectator, like the female subject, appears in 'male drag'. The mirror, the representational frame held 'up to life' is in male hands (see Dolan 1985a for further discussion of this point). As feminism rejects the formal and ideological apparatus which denies the female spectator a subject position, the case against the gaze of realism is clear.

The critique of the gaze surfaces again in Chapter 4 which examines the construction of Woman as 'Other' than Man in the context of French feminist theory. Later, in Chapter 7, questions of address and spectatorship are discussed in the context of feminist theatre practice which has intervened in the construction of the gaze to explore the possibilities of a 'female' subject positioning for the feminist spectator.

4

M/OTHERING THE SELF
French feminist theory and theatre

In a European context the representation of Woman as 'Other' than Man, as introduced in the previous chapter, has dominated French feminist theory. The three key exponents of this field are Hélène Cixous, Luce Irigaray, and Julia Kristeva. This chapter will outline the main concepts which have been 'borrowed' by feminist theatre studies from *écriture féminine* ('writing said to be feminine'), suggest why they have been important to feminist theatre, and how they have been taken up in critical practice (for an extended example of this, see the case study of Deborah Levy's *Heresies*, Chapter 9, pp. 124–7).

The reception of French feminist theory is complicated and complex because of primary levels of difficulty in the source texts, the problems attendant on their translation, and the critical readings of the theories which are sometimes based on partial, even misunderstood, readings of the original texts (see Irigaray 1993: 58–9). The reader who is new to this field of feminism, therefore, may find it useful to refer to the accessible edited volume by Marks and Courtivron (1981), and Moi's authored study (1985), Part Two of which surveys the work of Cixous, Irigaray, and Kristeva. (Moi's study is particularly useful because it places the surveys in a critical context, highlighting what have been the chief objections to the ideas and theories proposed.)

CIXOUS

Woman as the object of male exchange, of male desire, is critiqued in the theoretical writings of the French feminist Hélène Cixous. Cixous has been primarily identified with the binary opposition of Woman as 'Other' than Man, and as desirous of rejecting the logo-/phallo-centric structures which divide up the world according to sexual difference:

> Her whole theoretical project can in one sense be summed up as the effort to undo this logocentric ideology: to proclaim woman as the source of life, power and energy and to hail the advent of a new, feminine language that ceaselessly subverts these patriarchal binary schemes where logocentrism colludes with phallocentrism in an effort to oppress and silence women.
>
> (Moi 1985: 105)

The call for 'woman to write herself' (see Cixous's 'The Laugh of the Medusa', 1981 [1975]), to find her own 'language' out in the margins of male order(s) is a theoretical concept for which one can find parallels in women's theatrical practice. The recognition that phallocentric forms such as the 'prisonhouse of art', as Case calls realism (1988: 124), has similarly pushed women playwrights and practitioners towards a breaking up of forms and the possibility of what might be designated a 'female' style of practice. Such a view does attract criticism from feminists on the grounds of essentialism: for its potential failure to recognize that the concept of what is female has also been determined by patriarchy. However, the theorization of voice, subject, body, structure, etc. which French feminist theory proposes, is attractive to feminist theatre critics because it parallels the practical concerns of the performance context:

> For her theory of feminine writing – 'écriture féminine' – which she formulated just as she was beginning to move into theatre is particularly appropriate to a description of drama. 'Ecriture féminine', with its emphasis upon transformation and profusion and its reference to the corporal, provides a clarifying perspective through which to view performance and the relationship between performance and the written theatrical text.
>
> (Running-Johnson 1989: 179)

For 'woman to write herself' she needs to be re-located, un-made in the pre-Oedipal space of the Lacanian Imaginary, i.e. the presymbolic. Her voice is 'the Voice' that 'sings from a time before law, before the Symbolic took one's breath away and reappropriated it into language under its authority of separation' (Cixous and Clément 1987 [1975]: 93). It requires a bursting, a violent breaking up of the symbolic order/language which has denied women their 'voice', their identity:

> Voice-cry. Agony – the 'spoken' word exploded, blown to bits by suffering and anger, demolishing discourse: this is how she has always been heard before, ever since the time when masculine society began to push her offstage, expulsing her, plundering her. Ever since Medea, ever since Electra.
>
> (94)

There is a tendency when discussing concepts of a 'female voice' in contexts of academic debate, where French feminist theory is used to explicate theatrical text, to forget that Cixous's idea of the Voice is located in the *pre-Oedipal* stage: it is not 'female' in the sense accorded to this term in its binary, symbolic definition relative to the 'male'.

Modern women's theatre is characterized by a resistance to being pushed 'offstage' and is replete with explosions, 'demolishings' of discourse. In Churchill's *Top Girls*, for example, the final moments of the dinner scene might be described as marking the desire to exit from the symbolic. The dinner scene, as a whole, centres on a model of collective oppression in which the individual narratives of female objectification offered by the women from their different fictional, historical, 'real' planes constitute a radical critique of the Symbolic Order, its structures and ideologies. Diamond (1989), for example, comments on the use of costume to make 'visible' an historical/patriarchal text which is, however, a sight/site of disruption in terms of the 'spoken' pain and suffering:

> The five 'top girls' eating and drinking together in an expensive London restaurant have entered Western representation, but at a cost. Each points to the elaborate historical text that covers her body – Nijo in geisha silks, Joan in regal papal robes – but their fragmented speeches, the effect of the words of one being spoken through and over words of another, refer to need, violence, loss, and pain, to a body unable to signify within those texts.
>
> (266)

This crescendoes in the final moments to a chaotic 'closure'. Gret's anti-male warfare narrative swells to a collective anger shared by the female dinner guests. Pope Joan's spewing out of Latin (male language *par excellence*) is followed by her being physically sick. Nijo is 'laughing and crying' and 'Marlene is drinking Isabella's brandy' (Churchill 1984 [1982]: 28–9). The responses are emotional, physical, oral, chaotic. Only Isabella continues with her '"spoken"' narrative, but this is 'blown to bits' by the bodily responses of the other women. It is the voice which, in Cixous's terms, is 'unfastening' as 'she shoots away. Break. From their bodies where they have been buried, shut up and at the same time forbidden to take pleasure' (Cixous and Clément 1987 [1975]: 94).

Cixous herself proposed that the desire to exit from the symbolic in order for women to come out of silence was the first stage in the journey of modern women's theatre. In her short essay with the punning title 'Aller à la mer' (1984), 'go to the mother/sea', Cixous advocates that the return to the (pre-Oedipal) mother is the trajectory for women's theatre. Of theatre as it is she asks:

> How, as women, can we go to the theatre without lending our complicity to the sadism directed against women, or being asked to assume, in the patriarchal family structure, that the theatre reproduces *ad infinitum* the position of victim?
>
> (1984: 546)

The inability of woman to take up a subject position in theatre, and in particular the violence en-acted against women within the theatrical frame, meant that Cixous's own initial response to this question was to stop going to the theatre (546). Subsequently, however, Cixous wrote her own piece for theatre which was, as she describes it, emblematic of the desire for women to exit from the Symbolic Order of the theatrical frame. The piece was *Le Portrait de Dora*, which began life as a radio play (1972), and was subsequently adapted and directed by the French director Simone Benmussa at the Petit Orsay Theatre in 1976. Based on Freud's case study of Dora (a female patient who walked out on the case before Freud had completed his diagnosis of her 'illness'), the play is a staging of feminist interventions in psychoanalysis. Cixous describes the play as follows:

> *Le Portrait de Dora* was the first step for me in a long journey; it was a step that badly needed to be taken, so that a woman's voice could be heard for the first time, so that she could cry out, 'I'm not the one who is dumb. I am silenced by your

inablity to hear.' Again, this is a scene with the Father, but it is a scene in which the relationship is broken off; in the end Dora walks out, leaving the 'Vieux Je' (Old Ego/Old Hat) behind her. This journey takes her from dependence, through suffering, until she exits onto an entirely different stage/ scene.

(1984: 547)

Cixous's *Dora* has become a major reference point for feminism and psychoanalysis, as well as a theatricalization of French feminist theory. There have been numerous case studies of Cixous's *Dora* (for examples see Lamont 1989; Savona 1989; Willis 1990). However, there is a tendency to discuss the play within a psychoanalytical frame which threatens to undermine theatrical considerations and contexts. A more useful approach, from the point of view of theorized *practice*, would perhaps be to give more detailed consideration to Benmussa's production notes and the techniques and styles of staging which she proposes as a way of realizing the exit from the Father in a performance context: of translating the abstract concept into a staged 'reality' (see Benmussa 1979: 9–19). This might facilitate an understanding of performance techniques which, in the context of a 'feminine' aesthetic, could advance Cixous's concept of the return to the pre-Oedipal mother.

IRIGARAY

Cixous's contemporary Luce Irigaray has only recently been accorded a higher profile in British and American feminist debates. She is best known for her two publications in the 1970s: *Spéculum de l'autre femme* (1974) based on her controversial doctoral thesis (see Moi 1985: 127), and the collection of essays *Ce sexe qui n'en est pas un* (1977), both of which came out in long overdue translations in 1985 (*Speculum of the Other Woman* and *This Sex Which Is Not One*). The recently published *Irigaray Reader* (Whitford 1991) signals the diversity of her work: psycho-linguistics, critiques of psychoanalysis, philosophy, and, more recently, social forms (see Whitford's introduction for a more detailed overview). Although Irigaray's projects are wide-ranging and diverse, her post-Derridean activities of deconstruction (i.e. theories concerned with the unfixing of meaning, as proposed by the French philosopher Jacques Derrida; for a brief, accessible introduction see Reinelt and Roach 1992: 111–13) and feminist strategies of revisioning (whether linguistic, philosophical, pyschoanalytical, etc.), hold some common ground with Cixous's. As Moi comments, 'it is interesting to note that in spite of certain divergences, Irigaray's vision of femininity and of feminine language remains almost indistinguishable from Cixous's' (1985: 143).

Irigaray critiques the Western traditions of philosophy and psychoanalysis for the ways in which they have systematically relegated woman to a negative, non-subject, non-speaking position. Irigaray's proposal for the re-making of Woman is based on a return to the (sexual) pleasures of the body. In her essay 'The Sex Which Is Not One', Irigaray claims that woman's auto-eroticism has the capacity to be self-defining and non-mediated, unlike man's where he needs 'an instrument in order to touch himself: his hand, woman's genitals, language':

> A woman touches herself by and within herself directly, without mediation, and before any distinction between activity and passivity is possible. A woman 'touches herself' constantly without anyone being able to forbid her to do so, for her sex is composed of two lips which embrace continually. Thus, within herself she is already two – but not divisible into ones – who stimulate each other.
>
> (Irigaray 1981 [1977]: 100)

Irigaray's articulation of woman's desire which 'most likely does not speak the same language as man's desire' (101), is further located in the corporeal plurality of sexual pleasures. When woman speaks her pleasure/s:

> 'She' is indefinitely other in herself . . . 'she' goes off in all directions and in which 'he' is unable to discern the coherence of any meaning. Contradictory words seem a little crazy to the logic of reason, and inaudible for him who listens with ready-made grids, a code prepared in advance. In her statements – at least when she dares to speak out – woman retouches herself constantly . . . One must listen to her differently in order to hear an *other meaning' which is constantly in the process of weaving itself, at the same time ceaselessly embracing words and yet casting them off to avoid becoming fixed, immobilized* . . . Moreover, her statements are

never identical to anything. Their distinguishing feature is one of contiguity. They touch (*upon*). And when they wander too far from this nearness, she stops and begins again from 'zero': her body-sex organ.

(103)

Speaking the body/the body speaking, constitutes an attractive proposal for women's writing and performance in theatre. Josette Féral takes Irigaray's 'feminine discourse' and applies it to women's theatre texts, describing the 'feminine voice' as one characterized by 'simultaneity', which 'would transform meaning into a continuous flow within the text' (1984: 550). The movement of the text would be non-linear, moving 'in all directions at once', 'interwoven' like the body, avoiding definition (ibid.). One of the texts Féral examines in the light of Irigaray's idea of 'woman-speaking' is Sylvia Plath's *Three Women*. It is a poem for three women's voices which was broadcast as a radio play in 1962. Set in 'a maternity ward and round about' (Plath 1981 [1962]: 176), the three voices speak of their pains, joys, suffering of birth, and loss. These are not women who are represented as named wives, sisters, daughters. Their identity is not mediated through a male presence. The narrative is not fixed or singular. It is plural and woven out of the women's speaking of themselves, of their experiences which 'touch' each other, overlap, move away, return, etc. It is characterized by the traces of the writing/speaking voice said to be feminine:

Odd patches, unfinished sentences, mental shifts (contiguity), marking time, repetitions, flashbacks, hesitations, interjections, silences . . . It exemplifies a certain kind of feminine writing, a certain kind of woman-speech or simply speech, in which (according to Luce Irigaray) thoughts come together and separate, speech comes to a standstill and goes on, hesitates, backtracks and then starts off again, asks questions without expecting an answer or gives answers without asking questions, and sometimes interrupts itself for no reason, only to continue further on, different and always the same.

(Féral 1984: 558)

KRISTEVA

The third of the internationally acclaimed French feminists is the Bulgarian-born psychoanalyst and linguistician Julia Kristeva.

Again, critical presentations of French feminist theory tend to stress similarity and conceal difference. Moi's survey of Kristeva's work makes it clear, however, that unlike Cixous and Irigaray, Kristeva is resistant to the idea of a 'female' language (see Moi 1985: Chapter 8). Rather, her work on language as a 'complex signifying *process*', and 'the *speaking subject* as an object for linguistics', Moi explains (152), combines with her psychoanalytical studies to propose a 'theory of marginality' rather than 'femininity' (164).

The binary concept of the *semiotic* and the *symbolic* has in Kristeva's work become a touchstone in feminist theoretical writings on women's theatre. Kristeva's use of the term *semiotic* is quite different to the way in which semiotics/semiology is taken to designate the discipline and activity concerned with the signifying practices of sign-systems. Semiotic, in the Kristevan sense, is dependent upon an understanding of the 'split' subject. In psychoanalytic terms, Lacan's Imaginary and Symbolic Order are replaced by the *semiotic* and the *symbolic*: 'the interaction between these two terms then constitutes the signifying process' (Moi 1985: 161). The semiotic is identified with the pre-Oedipal phase and

> relates to the *chora*, a term meaning 'receptacle,' which she borrowed from Plato, who describes it as 'an invisible and formless being which receives all things and in some mysterious way partakes of the intelligible, and is most incomprehensible'.
>
> (Roudiez 1980: 6)

The repression of the *chora* is required in the *thetic* phase which marks the entry into the symbolic for meaning to be produced:

> The symbolic process refers to the establishment of sign and syntax, paternal function, grammatical and social constraints, symbolic law . . . The speaking subject is engendered as belonging to both the semiotic *chora* and the symbolic device, and that accounts for its eventual split nature.
>
> (ibid.: 6–7)

Kristeva's theorization of the semiotic and symbolic are bound up in her style of critical practice which explicates a wide range of cultural texts, including writing, painting, criticism (see Kristeva 1980), and 'modern theatre' (see Kristeva 1977). Kristeva's critical practice invites readings of texts as semiotic or symbolic. In a text which one might characterize as predominantly semiotic the signs of the *chora* will explode the symbolic, whereas in the symbolic text the *chora* is more severely (though not wholly) repressed. Theorizations of modern women's theatre have appropriated the Kristevan semiotic/symbolic in the interests of demonstrating women's drive towards the semiotic.

One early twentieth-century American playwright whose work has been re-framed and re-read in relation to the semiotic and the symbolic is Susan Glaspell, the subject of the case study in Chapter 8. Her theatre is paradigmatic of the drive towards the semiotic. Although Glaspell worked in a realist (i.e. Kristevan symbolic) mode of drama, she was nevertheless resistant to its logo/phallo-centric order. Her plays are formally and thematically encoded with 'otherness', borders, boundaries, edges, outside, etc. The 'lethal' semiotic 'drive of forgetfulness or of death' (Kristeva 1977: 132), is represented in the traces of absent/present 'heroines' who cannot take a place in the Symbolic Order. Glaspell's women constantly weave their 'text' out of 'undoing', 'unspeaking': signs of the semiotic pressing upon, disrupting, and fragmenting the symbolic:

> her plays speak to the same concerns that occupy feminist critics . . . And while Glaspell's struggles to create a female language do not go as far as those espousing *écriture féminine* would probably accept, they are predicated on some of the same beliefs: that women's subjugation in society is connected to the subjugation imposed by language.
>
> (Ben-Zvi 1989: 157)

There are a further two key ideas arising out of the Kristevan symbolic and semiotic which have been central to feminism and theatre: 'women's time', and *jouissance*.

In her essay 'Women's Time' Kristeva links female subjectivity to two 'types of temporality' which she identifies as 'cyclical' and 'monumental' (1982 [1979]: 35). She explains these two 'types of temporality' as follows:

> As for time, female subjectivity would seem to provide a specific measure that essentially retains *repetition* and *eternity* from among the multiple modalities of time known through the history of civilizations. On the one hand, there are cycles, gestation, the eternal recurrence of a biological rhythm which conforms to that of nature and imposes a temporality

whose stereotyping may shock, but whose regularity and unison with what is experienced as extrasubjective time, cosmic time, occasion vertiginous visions and unnameable *jouissance*. On the other hand, and perhaps as a consequence, there is the massive presence of a monumental temporality, without cleavage or escape, which has so little to do with linear time (which passes) that the word 'temporality' hardly fits.

(1982: 34)

Consequently, female subjectivity is therefore alienated from 'time as project, teleology, linear and prospective unfolding; time as departure, progression, and arrival – in other words, the time of history' (35). This is also, Kristeva explains, the time of language:

This linear time is that of language considered as the enunciation of sentences (noun + verb; topic–comment; beginning–ending), and, that this time rests on its own stumbling block, which is also the stumbling block of that ennunciation – death.

(ibid.: 35)

Kristeva links her analysis of time to three phases of feminism: 1. the struggles of the Women's Movement to have a recognized place in the linear time of history; 2. the refusal of linear time in the interests of finding 'the intrasubjective and corporeal experiences left mute by culture in the past'; 3. a synthesis of these 'two attitudes' (36–8).

In terms of women's theatre, feminist criticism has linked the concept of 'linear time' to those dramatic forms such as realism which are alienating to the female subject. Realist drama depends upon the purposeful interactive speaker–listener interchanges in which 'successful' acts of speaking drive action on through exposition, progression, and climax to a closure. The linearity of speaking time, ordered by units of dramatic time and action, therefore represses the 'speaking' of women's experiences.

In the quest for women's exeriences 'left mute by culture in the past', other critical approaches to theatre have highlighted the concept of the 'cyclical'. Gillian Hanna of Monstrous Regiment, for instance, described how the group's early work involved a refusal of linear structures which could not encompass women's experience:

If we look at the progression we've made through *Scum,*
Vinegar Tom, Kiss and Kill, it does seem that what we have
been pushing towards in all three is a kind of breaking up
of things. It's precisely a refusal to accept . . . that life is linear,
that it has a comprehensible beginning, middle and end,
which has to do with male experience. I think men experience the world like that. They are born into a world
where they can map out life. It has a beginning, a middle and
an end. It has a form, a shape. It has to do with a career. It
has to do with your work. With all of those things. Now for
a woman, life is not like that. It doesn't have that pattern. For
a woman life and experience is broken backed.

(Hanna 1978: 8)

Explorations into finding a form to represent the 'broken backed'
experience of women which has been repressed, necessitated the
explosion of the linear, the masculine. However, to be heard, such
a voice has to be located at some level in the symbolic, hence
Hanna's description is one of 'breaking up' forms rather than
speaking from 'outside' language.

Of the three plays Hanna cites, Churchill's *Vinegar Tom* (1985
[1978]) might, in particular, be argued for as a text which registers
Kristeva's third position: the need to enter linear time/history,
with a need for 'women's time'. *Vinegar Tom* is both historical and
monumental as a text. It combines an historical, oppressive past in
its subject of seventeenth-century witchcraft, with the monumental
temporality of patriarchal oppression, to articulate the marginality
of women. Churchill's work continues to explore women's position
in relation to an '*insertion* into history and the radical *refusal* of the
subjective limitations imposed by this history's time' (Kristeva
1982: 38), as evidenced in the collapsing and shifting of temporal-
ities in *Cloud Nine* (1979), *Top Girls* (1982), and *Fen* (1983). (For
further analysis along these lines see Diamond 1990.)

In order not to be a 'sick' child in Lacanian terms, entry into the
symbolic is required at some level to be able to communicate and
to make oneself understood. However, it is 'the revolutionary
subject, whether masculine or feminine', that 'is a subject that is
able to allow the *jouissance* of semiotic motility to disrupt the strict
symbolic order' (Moi 1985: 170). *Jouissance* is a term which tends
to be left untranslated as there is no concise way of translating
without betraying or reducing its meaning. Roughly, however, it

55

corresponds to a sense of 'total joy or ecstasy' and 'also, through the working of the signifier, this implies the presence of the meaning (*jouissance* = *j'ouïs sens* = I heard meaning), requiring it by going beyond it' (Roudiez 1980: 16). In Cixous's framework, for example, it is used to denote the pleasure of woman writing herself in the space of the pre-Oedipal, the pre-Symbolic. Moi explains how, in Kristeva's terms, the possibility of semiotic *jouissance* arises, and combines her explanation with textual examples:

> Since the semiotic can never take over the symbolic, one may ask how it can make itself felt at all. Kristeva's answer to this point is that the only possible way of releasing some of the semiotic pulsions into the symbolic is through the predominantly anal (but also oral) activity of *expulsion* or *rejection*. In textual terms this translates itself as a *negativity* masking the death-drive, which Kristeva sees as perhaps the most fundamental semiotic pulsion. The poet's negativity is then analysable as a series of ruptures, absences and breaks in the symbolic language, but it can also be traced in his or her thematic preoccupations.
>
> (Moi 1985: 170)

The examples which Kristeva uses and Moi summarizes are taken from the *avant-garde* poets and modernist writers. In the context of women's theatre it is the breaking up of dramatic dialogue, form, character, etc., which is analysed in relation to the semiotic and the possibility of *jouissance*. Griffin (1991), for example, analyses the 'semiotic disposition' of Ann Jellicoe's *The Sport of My Mad Mother* (1958), examines its potential for *jouissance* arising from the play's 'non-linear' structure, disruption of language techniques, use of percussion rhythms as a patterning device, etc. However, Griffin also uses this approach to demonstrate that the engendering of the text in its portrait of the teenage street gang, is such that the 'revolutionary potential' of the semiotic to disrupt the symbolic is constrained (1991: 37). (For a contrasting view see Thompson 1992.)

The surveying of French feminism in this chapter has been linked to feminist theatre texts and critical practice. In the next chapter, the section on radical/cultural feminism indicates the influence of 'writing said to be feminine' on experiments with a 'female' language, aesthetic, and acting style in feminist theatrical practice.

5

STAGING FEMINISM(S)

Contemporary feminist playwrighting and performance has reshaped the modern dramatic/theatrical canon, and signalled its difference from mainstream (male) theatre. A recently published survey of the British stage from 1890 to 1990 by Innes (1992), testifies to this difference by concluding with an (all too brief) section on the emergence of feminist companies and dramatists, kept separate from the main body of the (male) survey. Innes explains the rationale of this 'organizing principle' as being due to the way in which 'the feminist playwrights consciously reject conventional forms as inherently masculinist, and as a consequence their criteria demand separate treatment' (Innes: 7). He also states that it is in the context of emergent companies 'performing for special interest groups' that 'some of the more challenging new writing has emerged, the most highly developed being feminist drama' (ibid.). Innes's own emphasis is on the feminist playwrights (though he treats only two: Gems and Churchill), which reflects a traditional academic approach to theatre which prioritizes the dramatic at the expense of the theatrical. As a consequence, the consideration and documentation of the performance context suffers, because what gets written about are the plays – possibly reviewed in production, but rarely analysed for their performance style, staging potential, etc.

Feminist theatre studies, however, has attempted to place feminist drama in its performance context, theorizing both text and practice. This chapter aims to reflect this methodology: analysing the evolution of the feminist performance context in which the 'challenging new writing' has emerged over the past twenty years or more, and reversing the traditional emphasis on the plays/playwright. The chapter surveys the roots of a feminist theatrical practice in the companies emerging in the 1970s, examines how the different feminist dynamics (bourgeois, radical/ cultural, and socialist/materialist) have shaped theatre texts and performance contexts, illustrating each dynamic with a combination of textual and practical examples.

FEMINIST THEATRE GROUPS: THEORY AND PRACTICE

The context of the Second Women's Liberation Movement in the USA and Britain spawned a number of women's theatre groups who, in subsequent years, attracted a good deal of interest from feminist theatre scholarship (particularly in the States), seeking to theorize their practice. Articles on American women's theatre groups in the 1970s provided lists of who the groups were and where they were working (for an overview of such articles see Leavitt 1980: 21). Patti Gillespie, for example, cites 1969 as the year in which the first groups were formed, footnoting the dispute between the New Feminist Theatre (New York City) and the Los Angeles Feminist Theatre over claims to be the first (1978: 284). Dinah Luise Leavitt describes the rise of the groups as 'unique', claiming that there had 'never before been a feminist theatre' (1980: 99). That feminist scholarship rushed to claim this phenomenon as a 'first' risked perpetuating the historical invisibility of women's work in theatre (as discussed in Chapter 2). It overlooked the fact that the phenomenon of women seeking to create their own experimental 'space' in opposition to male-dominated theatre was nothing new (and, indeed, when further advances are made in the field of feminist theatre history, it will probably turn out to be as old as theatre itself). However, the misplaced sense that the feminist theatre groups in the 1970s constituted a new phenomenon was responsible for a documentation of their theatrical practice which might otherwise, like so much of women's culture, have gone unrecorded.

Among the early analysis of feminist theatre companies was an overview of American groups by Charlotte Rea (1972), which offered the following observation on the collective company structure:

> While the collective structure has been adopted by many feminists, their groups differ in one important aspect from

their male-dominated counterparts. This difference is the absence of a leader or director. Almost without exception, heterosexual groups evolve into a leader/followers political structure.

(79)

The absence of a 'leader or director' was noted in a rhetorically based analysis of the Liberation Movement by Karlyn Kors Campbell:

The rhetoric of women's liberation is distinctive stylistically in rejecting certain traditional concepts of the rhetorical process – as persuasion of the many by an expert or leader, as adjustment or adaptation to audience norms, and as directed toward inducing acceptance of a specific program or a commitment to group action. This rather 'anti-rhetorical' style is chosen on substantive grounds because rhetorical transactions with these features encourage submissiveness and passivity in the audience – qualities at odds with a fundamental goal of feminist advocacy – self-determination.

(1973: 78)

Campbell's article subsequently became a reference point for analysing the ways in which collective or group-based theatre created by women in the 1970s might share the rhetorical base of the Movement at large (for further discussion see Zivanovic 1989). What Campbell had identified was the 'consciousness raising' rhetoric of feminism which advocated collective self-determination by women, as opposed to the dominant rhetorical mode in which a single rhetorician persuades his listener(s)/audience to accept his argument. In turn, the feminist rhetoric of collectively organized women's theatre was argued for: 'all feminist theatres are rhetorical enterprises; their primary aim is action, not art' (Gillespie 1978: 286).

Janet Brown's 'definition and critical analysis' of 'feminist drama' (1979) identified four rhetorical devices common to feminist theatre which were used to challenge dominant representations of women:

1 the sex-role reversal device;
2 the presentation of historical figures as role models;
3 satire of traditional sex roles;
4 the direct portrayal of women in oppressive situations.

(1979: 88)

Categories 1 and 3 were described as using conventions of gender-based stereotyping in order to challenge and undermine them. The second device aimed to use historical figures in order to create a positive female image, and the fourth device was designed to show oppressive images of women in a critical light.

The notion of feminist theatre as a 'a study in persuasion' was developed in Elizabeth J. Natalle's full-length study (1985). Natalle explicates the rhetorical process as a communication model and provides a crude model of 'human communication': Source → Message → Receiver, with 'feedback' from Receiver to Source. This is developed by Natalle in a model of the 'feminist theatre phenomenon', designed to illustrate the points in the communication process 'where persuasion is likely to take place'. She establishes five such points:

1 in the period of research for a play when group members may need to interrogate their own feminist beliefs;
2 in the play as a feminist message;
3 in the collaboration of the audience in the feminist messages performed;
4 the act of performing as a further means of persuading the actresses of their feminist beliefs, and
5 both performers and the audience may be persuaded of feminist ideas in a post-performance discussion.

(see Natalle 1985: 14–15)

The rhetorical processes of collective persuasion, as identified somewhat crudely in Natalle's analysis, could be developed into a more theoretically grounded model if framed within current debate on speech-act theory applied to drama/theatre within the semiotic field of reception analysis (for an introduction to speech-act theory and drama, see Aston and Savona 1991, Chapter 4). Examination of the 'perlocutionary' effect of drama (i.e. the effect on the addressee/audience through what is said), as proposed by the semiotician Keir Elam, furthers an understanding of the ideological choices which go into a theatrical model. Elam proposes a table of 'some of the most important historical perlocutionary models of dramatic representation' from Aristotle to Brecht, though none of these 'important' models are woman-authored (Elam 1988: 51–3). The 'perlocutionary package' in the table comes in the last two elements: the 'perlocutionary object . . . or the effect of the communication on the audience, and the perlocutionary sequel ... the practical consequences of the act' (51). Hence, in some models of theatre the perlocutionary effect is concluded in the theatre. In others, like the Brechtian model for example, the perlocutionary effect is 'sequel-ended, founded on the ideal of a direct influence on posttheatrical social practice' (54). The feminist theatre group model of the 1970s desired such a 'sequel'. It was designed not only to persuade the addressee/ audience of feminist beliefs in the theatre, but also invited them to take action after the theatrical event, in order to ameliorate, or even revolutionize, the position of women in society.

That this was to be achieved by collaborative, non-hierarchical persuasion between performers and audience had implications for feminist theatrical practice. The impact of the collaborative principle can be considered in the three production stages: the research and rehearsal period, the performance, and the post-performance discussion/sequel.

Research and rehearsal period

The initial discussion stages of a feminist theatre group generally began with the particular issues a group wished to explore in their next show. Whether these required research or discussion or a combination of both of these, the aim would be to work through a very lengthy democratic decision process of what should be said or not said; what would be put in or left out. Artistic con-siderations were often a very secondary consideration to the feminist beliefs which a group wished to theatricalize. Jude Winter of the British lesbian theatre group Siren recollects this process:

> Originally, when we wrote a play, we'd sit down and ask, 'What do we want to say? What are the political points we want to make?' We even used to have columns for these points, and how we would say them. Then, last of all, we'd find a theatrical way to say them. The plays were so long at first because we kept saying things like 'You can't keep out that point because of this point.' It wasn't a question of what would work as a theatre piece but of how could we possibly not say that.
>
> (unpublished interview with Siren, 1989)

Given the political impulse behind this kind of theatrical work, it was often the case that the women joining a company did so for political rather than professional reasons. Leavitt, for example, describes how, in its formative years, the Minneapolis-based, lesbian–feminist group the Lavender Cellar was 'open to any lesbian–feminist who could devote time and energy to one production' (1980: 44). Women might also come from unorthodox performance backgrounds, as was the case with Siren, for instance, where the women had previously been performing in rock bands.

The collective consciousness-raising discussion which framed the research period would then inform the stages of workshopping, scripting, and rehearsal. The concept of collaboration meant that every group member could be equally involved in every stage of the process. This accounts for the large number of collectively devised pieces which groups setting out in the 1970s created. The early repertoire of the Women's Theatre Group, for example, consisted entirely of group-devised, issue-based shows for teenage and adult audiences (for details see Wandor 1986: 51–3). It was a process which, particularly in terms of writing, groups were later to adapt in way which took more account of strengths and weaknesses, recognizing that it might be advantageous to commission a writer, or to allow a performer to develop her musical skills rather than having to be a 'Jill-of-all-trades'. But, even with this streamlining, the spirit of co-operation and collaboration would remain an important factor and allow women to choose how to develop their work in an environment which they could trust to be supportive.

Performance

The collaborative style of discussion, devising, scripting, and workshopping, etc., meant that the dominant mode of theatrical presentation was an ensemble style which promoted the idea of a group of performers rather than a star performer. Moreover, it was important to achieve an interactive and interrogative mode of engagement with the audience in order to work up to the 'sequel' effect. This entailed posing questions in relation to a woman-centred issue. Techniques of persuasion were built into the many and varied theatrical devices and styles of engagement (see below) which were designed to get a feminist message across. A group might, for instance, use comedy, music, or cabaret to illustrate its feminist viewpoint.

The processes of theatrical communication sometimes involved the audience feeding their experiences on a particular issue into a performance context. Natalle overviews American examples of this which include the audience input into two productions by At the Foot of the Mountain: *The Story of the Mother* in which spectators were asked to contribute to the scenes and rituals focusing on mother–daughter relationships, and *Raped: a Woman's Look at Bertolt Brecht's 'The Exception and the Rule'* in which the audience could offer their thoughts, feelings, etc. on rape (1985 20–1). Natalle explains that:

> the testimony offered by the audience members is actually a form of evidence that is spontaneously incorporated into the message presented by At the Foot of the Mountain. One person's testimony serves as self-persuasion and as proof to other audience members.
>
> (21)

Monstrous Regiment worked in a similar way in their production of Dacia Maraini's *Dialogue Between a Prostitute and One of Her Clients* (1980) in which the boundaries between the performer and the audience were challenged as the performers repeatedly broke off the dialogue between a prostitute and her male client to invite the audience to express its views by participating in the discussion (for further details see Bassnett 1984: 463–4; Hanna 1991: lii–liii).

Post-performance discussion/sequel

Given the perlocutionary aims of this feminist theatre, desirous of convincing its addressee/audience beyond the theatre, it followed that many of the plays, though by no means all, were accompanied by a post-performance discussion. The opportunity to discuss and persuade, again in a mutually supportive, non-hierarchical dialogue between the spectators and the performers, was viewed as an integral part of the theatrical event, rather than as an afterpiece. The consciousness-raising style of discussion might also have included concrete advice for women on a particular issue. Britain's Spare Tyre whose first show *Baring the Weight* (1979), inspired by Susie Orbach's *Fat is a Feminist Issue* (1978), launched them on a theatrical career in women's size and health issues, not only provided women with the opportunity to talk about their feelings about body size and dieting, but made sure that women knew how to get follow-up advice from the Women's Therapy

Centre (London). The company liaised with the Therapy Centre and together they set up self-help groups for women to cope with eating disorders. Spare Tyre's therapy work was a way of effecting the 'posttheatrical sequel': of persuading women to act on eating and health matters. Organizing therapy sessions, running educational workshops in schools and colleges, or self-help styled workshops for women, as many of the groups did, was all part of securing a successful 'uptake' of the 'perlocutionary package'.

TOWARDS A FEMINIST AESTHETICS?

The description and analysis of the feminist theatrical model which desires to persuade its spectators to 'act', needs to be complemented and extended by more detailed understanding of the type of feminist 'impulse' which underpins it. As there is no one single view espoused by feminism, it follows that different routes and objectives will be proposed in the en-actment of persuasion, resulting in different styles of feminist theatrical writing and performance aesthetics. The most accessible and widely used framing of feminism(s) is, as Chapter 1 briefly outlined, via consideration of the three dominant positions: bourgeois, radical/cultural, and socialist/materialist.

Early critical attempts to consider how feminist plays were representative of one or more of these positions was presumably a necessary stage in feminist critical re-evaluation, though as a methodology it is reductive and descriptive: 'there have been some attempts by women critics to define "feminist theatre" or "feminist plays", and in some cases this has ended up with a rather lame assertion that anything about women is necessarily feminist' (Wandor 1986: 138). For example, in a recent survey of 'feminist theatre in Britain' Goodman works to a definition of feminist theatre as 'loosely (re)defined as theatre which works in some way to present positive images of women, or to improve the status of women in the theatre (even if written by men or produced by mixed-gender companies)' (Goodman 1993b: 68). The reader is left in a position of trying to make sense of statistical results appertaining to 'feminist groups (all feminist women), women's groups (all women), mixed groups with feminist politics, and mixed groups with left politics, fairly positive for women' (70). A more productive approach is Wandor's advocacy of seeking not to label but to 'evaluate the nature of the feminist dynamic', or dynamics (Wandor 1986: 138). Wandor's suggestion is made in relation to plays. However, the concept of 'feminist dynamic' can be applied both to theatrical texts and performance contexts in order to identify how the three dominant strands of feminist enquiry have been adopted and developed in methods and techniques of dramatic writing, and performance aesthetics.

Bourgeois feminism: performance and plays

The aim of the bourgeois-feminist dynamic is to persuade the spectator of the case for improving the position of women within society without any radical transformation of political, economic, or familial structures, etc. The empowerment of women through this route is to be achieved principally via progressive legislation in respect of women's rights. In terms of theatre specifically, this translates into the aim of seeing the increased promotion of women into those spheres of theatrical administration, management, and performance which have been traditionally dominated by men without radical alteration to theatrical power structures. In American theatre this is identified by feminist critics in, for example, the phenomenon of the New York advocacy groups – League of Professional Women in Theatre, Women in Theatre Network, Women's Project – who 'provide opportunities for their constituents to display their work in showcase productions and staged readings' (Dolan 1989a: 202). The aim is to 'showcase' women's talent in order to see it more prominently displayed in mainstream theatre.

That it is not possible to talk about a feminist or women's acting style in this context is due to the 'showcasing' technique. The promotion of women's talent can in no way be linked to the concept of exploring the possibilities of a 'feminine' or feminist aesthetic. Rather, the aim is to be accepted into the mainstream on mainstream (i.e. male) terms. An actress finding a piece to demonstrate her talent will inevitably look for performance material which offers a 'strong' (in the sense of 'meaty') woman's role, but one which in terms of form and ideological content can be assimilated into dominant artistic and political values. With regard to a style of acting, this will entail performing within the dominant traditions of mainstream theatre, the most significant of these being the Stanislavski-based 'method' of performance.

In terms of playwrighting there are a relatively large number of texts which are informed by the bourgeois-feminist dynamic. Mary Remnant explains this as follows:

> Since some admission of women into mainstream theatre as writers would seem to be inevitable, a compromise of some sort has had to be found. Plays by women which reinforce or seem to reinforce male values are acceptable. Even liberal feminism may be aired on stage. Women may be shown to be oppressed but the oppressor must be invisible, or women's ills must be blamed on ourselves as individuals, or as a sex, or sometimes on individual males if they are historical, 'foreign' or 'other' in some way.
>
> (1987: 9)

One of the ways in which bourgeois feminism appears to be staging feminist concerns, but in fact is really reinforcing male values, for example, is through the method of taking a strong female character as the subject of the drama. Typical is the collection of short plays by the Women's Project: *Women Heroes* (1986). The title is in itself indicative of its bourgeois-feminist dynamic: the success of women is measured on male (hero) terms. The introduction confirms this in its description of the pieces as celebrating 'the lives of notable, exceptional women', and their ability to offer 'strong character relationships' (Miles 1986: vii). (For examples of the bourgeois-feminist dynamic in a British context see Wandor on Luckham's *Trafford Tanzi*, 1986: 177, and the analysis of *Steaming* in Chapter 9, pp. 120–4.)

Radical/cultural feminism and performance texts

In contrast to bourgeois feminism, radical feminism claims that the promotion of women is not enough to end their oppression. A more radical re-assessment of society's organizational structures is required: one which deconstructs patriarchal dominance and advocates the primacy of women's position. The consequence of this approach has been to place greater emphasis on women's creativity, to the extent that it is now considered by some as the advocacy of a 'female counter-culture' (see Dolan on Echols, 1988: 6). In terms of theatre, this feminist dynamic has given rise to investigations into whether there is a 'female language', an aesthetic or acting style 'said to be feminine', etc.

Such questions are impossible to formulate in a 'showcasing' environment, but are supported by the collective structures of persuasion described in the first part of this chapter. The use of personal experience in the shaping of performance material followed from the consciousness-raising paradigm of the Liberation Movement. The sharing of personal experience in a supportive group of women might form part of the pre-performance discussion period, and subsequently become part of the theatrical material evolved through workshopping and devising processes. Spare Tyre has commented:

> Our position ... was: if it's happened to us, it's probably happened to other women, too. So, for about the first five or six years, everything we did (except for a song about anorexia) was based on things which had happened to us or to friends of ours.
>
> (unpublished interview 1989)

The use of personal material by groups like Spare Tyre tended to feed predominantly into an issue-based style of performance which would en-act 'the personal as political' through a cross-media range of skills: song, music, comedy, drama, etc. (see below on socialist feminism and performance). There was, however, another strand of theatre emerging in which the personal was used to explore the possibilities of a 'new' gender-based performance style. Leavitt, writing on the American groups for instance, states that although collective organization was not in itself new, it had led to a 'new awareness' which centred on the possibility of a 'women's acting method' (1980: 101). She cites Circle of the Witch and At the Foot of the Mountain who argued that a difference in acting style for men and women could be rooted in the gender-based processes of socialization. Such groups Leavitt claims were 'in the process of discovering and identifying ... a method based on women's emotional responses to their personal experiences such as memories, dreams and wishes' (ibid.). The workshopping and performing of material in which the 'subject' for the performer is 'herself' clearly constitutes a radical break with traditional methods which insist that she enter into and identify with a character other than herself. Second, individual personal experiences of one woman may feed into areas of experience which are recognized as common to women and which enable a collective response: the experience of menstrual cycles or giving birth, for instance. Following this line, it may then be possible to investigate the possibilities of a gender-based ritual-ized style of theatre which seeks the emotional, mythical, and historical keys to a woman-centred culture.

The legacy of the radical-feminist dynamic, evolving in 'female counter-cultural' contexts, may be illustrated with two examples in which the theatrical text is 'scripted' by the female body: women's performance art, and the experimental work of the international Magdalena Project.

'Speaking the body': women's performance art

'Speaking the body' is a dominant element of contemporary women's performance art which has developed a particularly strong tradition in America. Case describes Carolee Schneeman's *Interior Scroll* (1975) in which the script of the performance was pulled out of the performer's vagina. One possible reading of this, Case suggests, is that it performs 'Irigaray's concept of beginning with the body organ in the production of female form' (1988: 58). However, feminist objections to women's performance art of this kind are raised because 'these performers fail to see that the female body is still a sign which, when placed in representation, particip-ates in a male-oriented signifying practice' (Dolan 1988: 83). One counter-argument to accusations of essentialism is the revisioning of the spectator–performer relations and the use of a 'private space'. That such performances were held in private spaces, for invited women, challenged the traditional hierarchy of the female body on public display for male consumption. Whereas the female body displayed in a private space for the 'female gaze' can also be critiqued for its endorsement of 'femaleness', it might also, how-ever, open up to the kind of 'speaking the body' which Irigaray proposes, and find new pathways for women's creativity, reclaim-ing the female body as a site of pleasure for women.

More recent women's performance art has taken on a harder edge and moved back into the public spaces of the American clubs and theatres. Performance artist Lenora Champagne still argues, however, for the medium 'with its use of explicit revelations and imagery' to 'provoke and shock audiences out of their com-placency' (1990: xii). Like Schneeman in the *Interior Scroll* the performance artist, Champagne claims, still scripts herself 'from a deep dark place'. Her final statement in the introduction to her anthology of texts by different American women performance artists resonates with the French feminist concept of speaking and writing the body:

> We're looking into ourselves, looking at the world around us, and letting our monsters out. Listen for the rage; you'll hear it. Listen again, and you'll hear laughter – the light side of the dark, the surplus of pleasure from that powerful release.
>
> (1990: xiii)

The Magdalena Project: from the 'personal' to the 'political'

Seeking the keys to a women's culture(s) and theatrical practice(s) is central to the on-going work of the international Magdalena Project whose home base is Cardiff, Wales. The project was inaugurated in 1986 by Jill Greenhalgh who invited thirty-eight women from fifteen different countries to participate in a three-week festival. Behind the idea of bringing together women from different European theatre groups was Greenhalgh's desire to see what would happen when she took 'all these women from their male directors for a period of collaboration' (Greenhalgh 1992: 107). Central to the first project were the explorations into women's creativity, trying to see whether it was distinct from 'male art' (see Speakman 1991: 19). Out of that first project arose a commitment to investigate theatrical practice rooted in women's experience:

> All this exchange, contact and stimulation opened a Pandora's box of realisations. Many of the women acknowledged, that for too long they had been complying with their directors to create a male art and not an art which reflected their experience. The release of this energy led to the founding of the Magdalena as an ongoing project committed to creating events and projects that would allow the questions that arose to be confronted in more detail and more depth.
>
> (Greenhalgh 1992: 108)

To suggest that the radical/cultural-feminist dynamic was the only impulse behind the first, and indeed subsequent, Magdalena projects would be misleading. Bassnett's account of the early stages of the Project's inception highlight the very different positions and beliefs which the women participants held, and, at times, hotly debated:

69

Whilst there was a group that could be designated as 'feminist' in the widest sense of the term, there was also another group of women, many of whom were actively involved in peace camps, whose starting point was an absolute belief in a separate female/feminine creative process. This group which tended to exalt the image of woman as mother, as human incarnation of the Great Mother, the Ultimate Creator of all things, often stood at the opposite pole to the feminists. So, for example, in a discussion on what kind of images should be presented in a women's theatre, one group wanted to glorify and develop images of domesticity and caring, whilst the other group wanted to reject all such images as typifying the history of women's confinement to the home and oppression in the world outside it. Likewise, whereas one group looked to images based on cyclical movements, on phases of the moon and menstrual rhythms, the other group rejected these as symbolic of the biological constraints that restrict the free movement of women in the world.

(Bassnett 1989a: 68–9)

However, the question of a 'female language' in theatre remained on the agenda. Two conferences held in Cardiff in September and December 1987 posed the question 'A Women's Language in Theatre?' Greenhalgh's aims for the second of these included the tentative suggestion that 'perhaps we can begin to identify some vocabulary that has some universal resonance for women – perhaps not. The work of this project is to find out' (quoted in Bassnett 1989a: 98).

The first production to come out of the Magdalena Project was the devised piece *Nominatae Filiae* (1988), directed by Sophia Kalinska, founder of Poland's first all-women's theatre group Akne Theatre. The question of female creativity is fundamental to Kalinska's work, and the interrogation of female archetypes is central to her explorations. Kalinska works from the belief that a woman's language lies in 'an international language to which we can gain access through a study of myths, symbols and archetypes' (Caplan 1991: 16). She states:

Women work in a different way. I try to encourage them to be more open, to find the truth about themselves. To express the things they have never been allowed to express before – power, anger, love. To break the stereotypes. To find their own creativity. It's no fun being a mere figure on a chess board, is it?

(Kalinska quoted in Caplan 1991: 17)

Nominatae Filiae, for example, looked at five archetypal images: Medea, Salome, the Little Mermaid, Miss Havisham, and Cassandra (for details and illustrations see Bassnett 1989a: 109–20). Kalinska's recent productions with the Nottingham-based company Meeting Ground have continued to investigate the *femme fatale* archetype, firstly in *The Sale of the Demonic Women*, and subsequently in *Plaisirs d'Amour*, a piece based on the story of Abelard and Heloise, although the lovers are reshaped by Kalinska to reverberate with echoes and images of John the Baptist and Salome.

One of the concluding observations in Caplan's piece on Kalinska's work is that 'where there is no fixed text, and the material is the stuff of women's most traumatic experiences, there is considerable danger' (Caplan 1991: 18). Where, as Caplan continues, 'the "poor" theatre calls upon the performer's most profound resources', then 'the dividing line between some of the work and madness is a fine one', and Caplan quotes Kalinska's admission to using '"psycho-drama, hysteria, trance"' (ibid.). It does raise questions, as Caplan suggests, of how to protect the performer. Moreover, the radical/cultural-feminist aesthetic is one which has been regularly critiqued for its essentialist position: for 'conceptualizing a female body-scene that keeps offstage political and material differences within and between genders' (Diamond 1989: 259). One director/performer who has become a regular workshop leader with the Magdalena Project and who provides ways of working through both of these problematics is the Argentinian director Cristina Castrillo. Castrillo's method of training the use of the 'personal' in workshop and performance contexts provides a way of 'protecting' the performer and also a means of keeping the political 'onstage'.

In the theatre training developed by Castrillo, the performer creates theatre through the twin development of the physical and emotional memories. The physical training and control is necessary to sustain the performer's emotional memory out of which s/he creates theatre. Castrillo writing on her role as director states:

> If I distinguish certain rules, I know that I perceive them united with the same rules that the actors practise in their own work: the use of tensions, oppositions, changes of

direction in the space, stops; the use of the emotional memory, etc.

They are surely the platform on which and through which the basic structure of a show manifests itself; the combination of contrasting values, sensations, lines, words, bones over which the physical and emotive presence of an actor should manifest itself, a structure which contains the personal logic of the emotional memory and the individual logic of the physical images eminating [sic] from that memory.

(Castrillo 1992: 3)

In the practice of Castrillo's theatre the performer is required 'to let the pressure out', to find creativity from the emotional memory within, and to realize these through the body (these explanations were given by Castrillo in her workshop for the Magdalena Project 'A Step Outside', Bristol, March 1990). As the performer is required to find her/his personal her/history as a starting point in creative theatrical practice, the personal memory is bound up in her/histories of gender, race, culture, etc., and these will be recalled and enter the theatrical frame. For example, the publicity for Castrillo's own solo performance in 'A Step Outside' stated:

Of her performance *Sobre el Corazon de la Tierre* [*On the Heart of the Earth*] Cristina says 'This performance recounts the aspects of life that come only from the realisation of death. To meet death means to value the most fundamental ways of feeling alive. The small life and death stories that make up this work originate from a history that is not simply personal'. These stories are deeply linked to the history of Cristina's people, her country, and to a collective past.

Castrillo's mirror exercise provides further illustration of this. The mirror is given to the performer as an object to react to. The exercise is set up so that there is little time to think. The performer is required to *feel* her/his response. In the Bristol workshop, where all the participants were women, the mirror prompted a range of vocal and physical responses which shared a pattern of dissatisfaction with appearance – sometimes playful, sometimes distressing – but, overall, refusing the authorship of the 'gaze'. In another exercise, personal herstories were recalled by using a highly-valued personal object and working off the emotional responses it triggered. The personal response on its own is not enough, the physical memory is needed to keep it controlled so that it can be performed: can be shown and shared with others. The female body in this context is not used as a reification of women's creativity, but as a means of siting personal herstories which may have been culturally, socially, and politically repressed.

Socialist/materialist feminism: practice and playwrighting

Both the bourgeois- and radical-feminist perspectives have been critiqued by the socialist/materialist-feminist position which seeks to locate oppression in terms of the complex matrix of gender, class, race, ideology, etc., and identify the historical sitings of such oppressions in order to radically transform society. In terms of theatre, the acting method which was widely adopted by feminist groups in the 1970s to demonstrate this was a method based on the theory and practice of Brechtian theatre, whose anti-illusionistic performance aesthetic challenged the form and ideological content of the classic realist tradition (see Chapter 3). This section will survey the development of a tradition of British feminist theatrical practice and playwrighting rooted originally in socialist/Marxist politics and the Brechtian style, and which subsequently, during the 1980s, provided a political and aesthetic framework, on both sides of the Atlantic, for materialist-feminist explorations of gender (the subject of Chapter 7). The socialist-feminist dynamic is explored through two illustrations: the initial Brechtian-styled practice of Britain's long-running socialist-feminist company, Monstrous Regiment; and a sampling of feminist playwrighting in the socialist tradition which dramatizes class politics.

A socialist-feminist theatrical practice: Monstrous Regiment

In the first wave of staging socialist-feminist debate, feminist practitioners generally regarded it as important to include men as part of the performance: the gender bias had to be argued through with men in order for them to be convinced of women's oppression and the need for change. It was also part of the socialist-feminist's journey in theatre. Women often had the experience first of working in a mixed, socialist company, of having to come to terms with the gender bias operating within that structure, and later moved into women-only, feminist companies. Hanna, for example, founder member of Monstrous Regiment, has explained how the company was formed because the socialist company Belts and Braces for whom she was working had no interest in finding the space for feminist interests in the company's work (see Hanna 1989). That said, Monstrous, in its formative years, included a minority of men in the company in the phase of socialist-feminist exploration:

> We sometimes get accused of having needed the sanction of the male presence at the beginning, but it wasn't about that. We were very clear about the fact that it was not about us feeling that we could not do it on our own. It had to do with recognizing that there were certain issues which we wanted to deal with on the stage which, in terms of how we thought about them, were also hangovers from our socialist pasts. We used to talk about 'the point of production': the point of production was where conflict occurred, that was the pinnacle of political activity, that was where it all happened. We sort of transported that into the relationship between men and women. We felt that that was where it was at, that was what was terribly and desperately and urgently needed examining and pulling apart.
>
> (unpublished interview: 1990)

Elsewhere, Hanna has explained her view of women's condition as one of alienation: 'I think most men are unaware of how alienated women feel. You are born into a world which belongs to somebody else, it doesn't belong to you. It belongs to men'(1978: 4). It was women's experience of alienation that informed the company's sense of what their theatre should look like. Uncovering history from a feminist perspective was the impulse behind their first two productions. *Scum* (1975) by Claire Luckham and Chris Bond, 'a musical celebration of the events of the Paris commune of 1871', linked the demands of the women in the Paris commune to the demands of women in the Liberation Movement of the 1970s. The Brechtian legacy emerges in the play's gestic techniques of disruption such as the use of song, direct audience address, and narrative structure, etc. Churchill's *Vinegar Tom*, which the company staged the following year, was also structured out of naturalistic scenes intercut with modern songs to examine witchcraft in the context of women's contemporary experience:

What we were saying about witchcraft was not necessarily true only of witchcraft, but of women's experience today. We had a very real feeling that we didn't want to allow the audience to get off the hook by regarding it as a period piece, a piece of very interesting history.

(Hanna 1978: 9)

The gestic style of *Scum* or *Vinegar Tom* called for what Hanna describes as a 'long-distance' method of acting (ibid.: 6) which could demonstrate the material conditions of a gender- and class-based oppression.

Class politics: an issue for socialist-feminist playwrighting

In the wake of the Liberation Movement the staging of class politics became an important issue for feminist playwrighting in Britain. The class-based character of British society and culture made a re-evaluation of class politics a vital part of socialist-feminist theatre, far more so in Britain, for example, than in the United States (see Case 1988: 84).

During the 1970s feminism scrutinized the theory and practice of socialism/Marxism for its gender bias, arguing that it had not taken account of sex-based oppression in its analysis of class relations. Feminists began to locate the oppression of women in their wageless work in the home and their reproductive labour for capitalism (see Hartmann 1979). In the theatre, the 'unhappy marriage' of Marxism and feminism provided the subject for several socialist-feminist plays. Brecht's *The Mother*, which had examined the 'mother's' oppression solely in class terms, was taken as a model for investigating women's oppression on account of class *and* gender. Typical was the socialist company Red Ladder's first 'women's play', *Strike While the Iron is Hot* (1972). Thrashing out the gender-bias of socialist politics began with the women in the company having to argue the low-priority given to women's issues by the men in the company (see Rawlence 1980: 17), just as Hanna had attempted to do with Belts and Braces. This in turn was gestically theatricalized in their Brechtian styled montage of scenes and songs which demonstrated the exploitation of its heroine Helen, both in the workplace and in the home (for further detail and discussion see Reinelt 1990).

Where the first phase of critiquing the 'unhappy marriage' of

75

Marxism and feminism concentrated on class relations between men and women, analysis of intra-sexual class oppression became a dominant feature of socialist-feminist playwrighting of the 1980s, as feminism had a 'new' oppressive factor to contend with: the 'Superwoman'. Thatcherite politics promoted the image of the high-flying female achiever who was capable of transcending class boundaries and of attaining material success at home and in the workplace. The reality was somewhat different. Very few women were in a position to gain access to paid positions of power which would enable them to combine work and family life.

This issue was centrally taken up in Churchill's theatre during the 1980s. *Top Girls* (1982) directly critiqued the 'Superwoman' ethos by demonstrating that the success of 'top girl' Marlene is achieved at the expense of oppressing her working-class sister Joyce, who has care of Marlene's daughter, Angie. The following year, Churchill's *Fen* offered a critique of capitalism and its effects on the working-class community of East Anglia's Fenlands. The women in Churchill's *Fen* are shown to be doubly oppressed: both as workers and as women. The critique of capitalist production and class exploitation is coupled with an examination of intra-sexual oppressive power relations: between the woman who is the overseer of the gang of women workers, and the women in the gang; in the violent step-mother/daughter relationship between Angela and Becky, etc.

Foregrounding the working-class woman's oppression as different to that of women from the upper and middle classes was also a feature of socialist-feminist drama in the 1980s based on an identity politics of regionalism. Thatcherite politics divided the country between the haves and havenots; between the prosperous south and the declining industrial north. Women in northern communities who had not benefited from the feminist movement, and had only limited access to the workplace, more often than not in low-grade, low-paid jobs, suffered increasing hardship as the wives of unemployed working-class men, and the mothers of children with jobless futures.

Plays in the 1980s which dramatized issues of class and gender oppression from a regional base include *Red Devils* (1983) by Debbie Horsfield, which is set in Manchester and examines the plight of jobless teenage girls; *About Face* (1985) by Cordelia Ditton and Maggie Ford, which is set on the Nottinghamshire/Derbyshire border and theatricalizes the women's involvement in the miner's strike of 1984–5; *Thatcher's Women* (1987) by Kay Adshead, which takes place in Manchester and London and dramatizes the issue of working-class women from the north of England travelling down to London to work as prostitutes in order to provide for their families.

The brutality of the 1980s for working-class women was most starkly and hard-hittingly demonstrated in the work of the teenage dramatist Andrea Dunbar, whose first play *The Arbor* was written when she was fifteen. Dunbar died suddenly in 1990 of a brain haemorrhage, but had written a further two plays, *Rita, Sue and Bob Too* (1982) and *Shirley* (1986), which continued her raw, harsh look at the lives of young, northern women (see Dunbar 1988). It was a style of theatre which the Royal Court company, who 'discovered' her and worked on all of her plays, termed the 'New Brutalism'. (The Court, also the 'home' of Churchill's work is, exceptionally, one of the few British theatres to give a high priority to class politics.) Again, Dunbar's work had a regional base. She wrote directly from her own experience of life on a council estate in Bradford in the industrial north of England: her characters are all drawn from her own working-class community. While her plays foreground the oppression of working-class men and women, the oppression of women is shown to be the greater, as the working-class men in their lives are also their (often violent) oppressors. Each of Dunbar's three plays conclude with women-only bonding scenes in which women have decided they are better off without men (for further details see Aston 1993b).

The alienated position of the working-class woman in relation to the feminist movement has not been the only critical voice inside, or, perhaps more accurately outside, the Women's Movement as the voices of the Black female practitioners in the following chapter demonstrate.

6

BLACK WOMEN
Shaping feminist theatre

AIN'T I A WOMAN

During the initial phase of feminist activity in the 1970s the emphasis of the Women's Liberation Movement was on 'sisterhood': the 'sameness' of women collectively oppressed by men. In urging women to recognize their 'universal' oppression the Movement advocated self-definition, but tended to overlook the historically determined material conditions of gender, race, class, and sexuality. A later phase of the Movement's history was, therefore, characterized by a 'breaking-up', a fragmentation, as working-class women, women of ethnic backgrounds of all classes, lesbians, and so on, sought to identify their different experiences of oppression which the white, middle-class, heterosexual Movement had overlooked:

> Lesbians in the movement pointed to the fact that heterosexual women had dominated and defined the agenda on sexuality . . . Black women wrote about how they had been silenced, and challenged the racist assumptions behind the almost universally accepted white feminist positions on violence against women, the family and reproductive rights . . . Women with disabilities, Jewish women and other 'identity groups' began to raise issues particular to their experience and like Black and lesbian women, claimed their own right to organize autonomously.
>
> (Harriss 1989: 35–6)

In the case of Black women specifically, their experience of oppression was and is triply grounded in gender, class, and race. The failure of the Movement to examine racial difference as part of its agenda has been challenged in the writings of the Black American activist bell hooks. In her first full-length study, *Ain't I a Woman* (1982), hooks claims:

> Initially, black feminists approached the women's movement white women had organized eager to join the struggle to end sexist oppression. We were disappointed and disillusioned when we discovered that white women in the movement had little knowledge of or concern for the problems of lower class and poor women or the particular problems of non-white women from all classes. Those of us who were active in women's groups found that white feminists lamented the absence of large numbers of non-white participants but were unwilling to change the movement's focus so that it would better address the needs of women from all classes and races.
>
> (1982: 188)

hooks continued her critique of the feminist movement in a further full-length study (1984), arguing that feminist theory needed to re-shape its aims and directions by looking to the women it had left out in the 'margins' of its dominant, white, middle-class 'centre'. In her opening chapter, 'Black Women: Shaping Feminist Theory' she explains:

> It is essential for continued feminist struggle that black women recognize the special vantage point our marginality gives us and make use of this perspective to criticize the dominant racist, classist, sexist hegemony as well as to envision and create a counter-hegemony. I am suggesting that we have a central role to play in the making of feminist theory and a contribution to offer that is unique and valuable.
>
> (1984: 15)

Throughout the 1980s the critical voices of Black women in America and Britain have established a critique of white feminist theories, causing some white feminists to address the racism of the Women's Movement (for a referencing of work in this field see Parmar 1989: 57). Similarly, feminist theatre of the early 1970s was also dominated by white, middle-class women, whose theatre was not representative of, for example, working-class white women, or Black women from any class background, etc. The white 'centre' of feminist theatre has been re-thought by some white feminist practitioners in the 1980s, while Black women have also 'shaped feminist theatre' by creating their own 'spaces' to write their materially conditioned histories of oppression into theatrical contexts.

Case's chapter on 'women of colour and theatre' in America acknowledges the difficulty for a white feminist author writing on race and class from a position of race and class privilege (1988: 95). The author is at the 'centre' writing on the 'margins'. I, similarly, wish to acknowledge that difficulty in presenting the material in this chapter and in the case study which accompanies it (Chapter 10). Not to document this work would, however, constitute a regressive return to a white, racist agenda of feminist theory and practice, and ignore a new direction in feminist theatre studies. It is also important that this 'theory' chapter and the accompanying case study are not read as segregated, marginal, 'colonized' spaces, but as 'centres' of theorized practice re-shaping feminist theatre. Moreover, in presenting the documentation in this chapter, I have tried to include as much material as I can from verbal (interview) and written sources by Black women, in order to marginalize my own white 'voice' (on this point see Goodman 1993a: 150). I have also included comments from white feminist practitioners who, acknowledging the movement's failure, have been seeking to address the racism of feminist theatre.

Case further acknowledges the difficulties of obtaining 'materials on ethnic feminist theatre practice' (1988: 95), and defines the parameters of her study as 'sampling' the theatre of 'two specific ethnic communities' in America (96): Black women and theatre, and chicanas in theatre (on the latter see also Yarbro-Bejarano 1990). This chapter is rooted in a British context, but is not bound by specific ethnic communities. Rather, the 'sampling' is concerned with the experience of Black women working in feminist theatre, and Black women creating theatre which gives expression to their identity as Black women living in Britain, and whose social and cultural experiences, unlike those of their white 'sister' feminists, are bound up in the colonizing histories of the Black diaspora (see Chapter 10, p. 135-6).

WHITE 'SPACES': BLACK WOMEN

Where white feminists have created their own performance group, space, or network, one of the key difficulties has been the breaking down of class and racial barriers in order to engage creatively with staging difference. Such attempts have not always been successful. In the Magdalena 1986 project, for example, protests were made about the possible elitism of the theatre the women were making and performing in terms of class and race. With regard to colour, accusations of racial prejudice were raised:

> One issue that recurred several times in reviews (*Spare Rib* took up this point, for example) was the small number of women of colour who took part in the proceedings. Jill Greenhalgh was questioned about why there were no African women performers, and although she explained that African women had been invited but had been unable to accept the invitation, charges of racial prejudice remained on the table. On the night of the final performance one woman, who had taken part in Phase 1, staged a protest about the absence of women of colour, suggesting that this had been deliberate policy rather than accidental.
>
> (Bassnett 1989a: 68)

The inability of African women to 'accept the invitation' was mainly financial, though it was also the case that the Project, at that time, had relatively few contacts with women in Africa. In 1987, it was possible for the Project to host a performance of *You Strike the Woman, You Strike the Rock* by the South African women's group the Vusiwe Players, because the company was already touring Britain and a booking was financially viable. (That the issue of the Project's networking with South African women has since been addressed is evidenced in the Project's current plans to host a Magdalena event in Zimababwe in 1994.)

The Magdalena example serves to show how feminist networks or companies seeking to engage Black women in their white 'spaces' have had to take active steps to change the all-white composition of their membership – chiefly through the implementation of policy changes which would positively discriminate in favour of Black women. Two groups which have worked in this way are the Women's Theatre Group, and the Birmingham-based Women and Theatre company.

The Women's Theatre Group introduced its multi-racial policy in 1985 which reads as follows:

1 This company, in all future appointments to company membership, shall work towards a racial composition

which is never less than 50% Black, and that having achieved this level it is maintained.

2 It is a minimum requirement that at least one out of every two of the companies writing commissions should be to a Black woman.

3 It is a minimum requirement that within each calender year 50% of free-lance jobs shall be offered to Black women.

4 This company commissions in equal ration:
a) Plays which while they can be about any subject must be performable by this company with its given racial composition.
b) Plays which whilst they can be about any subject must prioritise the lives and experience of Black women.

Setting up a policy, however, is not as easy as fulfilling it, as the company have been all too aware. In 1989 the Women's Theatre Group confirmed their commitment to their multi-racial policy by performing their first all-Black production *Zerri's Choice* by Sandra Yaw, but still needed to find ways of maintaining the involvement of Black women in the company other than writing and performing. Jenny Clarke, an administrator for the company at the time, outlined the problems as follows:

> We hope to have developed new audiences through the production of *Zerri's Choice*. Our multi-racial policy has always been very important and we're trying very hard to pursue it actively. It can be difficult to find people from different racial backgrounds to fill specific jobs we have vacant. For example, Jacqueline Fari, our Black technician, left to go on maternity leave and isn't coming back which is a real pity. We've been looking for a Black woman – Black in the broad political sense, meaning non-white – to replace her but have not been successful. This has partly to do with the fact that Jacqueline's replacement would have to be willing to go on tour. We've had a similar problem in finding a Black administrator.
>
> We feel that the way forward is to offer training to Black women in specific areas of work. In the recent past we have established a training programme for a Black designer, and are currently training a Black stage manager. We also plan to pursue this programme for an administrator.
>
> (unpublished interview, 1990)

Women and Theatre has also tried to move from its all-white beginnings in 1985 to a multi-racial position which would mean more than simply employing Black actresses. Founding-member Jo Broadwood admitted that this was difficult to achieve:

> When we decided to introduce ... changes to the group at Christmas 1989, we also talked about the way in which we were an all-white company and the way in which the management committee was all-white. We decided that we wanted to look at that in various ways. This is hard on lots of different levels because it shouldn't have to be just about employing Black actresses, it's also about making sure that our management committee has Black women represented on it. So we've been trying to take steps to ensure that that's happened. There is another difficulty in terms of finance: if you are one of the three core members of the company you want to be in work and performing in a project. This unfortunately encourages the sense of a Black actress carrying the banner for the whole Black community, and it shouldn't be forced upon them. We're trying to rectify that, but it is hard.
>
> (unpublished interview 1989)

Black actresses working for both of these feminist companies experience difficulty in negotiating race and gender in their performances. Areas of difficulty experienced include, for example, playing a 'white' role as a Black woman. In the Women's Theatre Group's production of Julie Wilkinson's *Pinchdice and Co.*, based on women in the crusades, casting in terms of race was important to the (white) playwright:

> It is quite important that in both productions Kisspenny was played by a black actress, and so was Cleverlegs whereas Pinchdice and Eleanor were both white. This is fairly obvious anyway from the references to their various origins in the script, perhaps least so in Kisspenny's case. The reason why this is important at all is because it adds another layer of significance for contemporary audiences to the growing relationship between Kisspenny and Cleverlegs.
>
> (Wilkinson, quoted in Aston and Griffin 1991a: 15)

However, Deb'bora John-Wilson who played the part in the Women's Theatre Group's production in 1989 felt, as a Black female performer, that the role of Kisspenny was a white role to which she had to bring her own Black identity in order to make it work for her as a performer: to make it a Black role:

> As a Black actress in *Pinchdice and Co.* I went back to things that were recognizable just to get through it because I was stuck. I know that there are things that I do as a Black person and can use in performance – my voice, for example . . . I didn't feel that my part was a Black part, so I basically started putting things on to Kisspenny and making stereotypes to make her Black.
>
> (unpublished interview, 1989)

Lorna Laidlaw, who took over a role which had been played by a white woman in Women and Theatre's production of *Putting it About* (1989), talked about the 'double negative' which the 'colour' dimension brings to a female role, and the difficulties which the performer encounters in terms of racial stereotyping:

> The character I'm playing for Women and Theatre was played before me by a white actress. So colour isn't a key factor, though of course, my playing the role does introduce a different dimension into it because of my colour. As with being a woman, being Black means there is a negative image to work against or break down.
>
> For example, when I was working with Big Brum, a mixed TIE [Theatre in Education] company in which I was the only woman, I'd feel very conscious of both my gender and colour when going into schools. (Interestingly, it either used to be me, as the only woman, or the one white male in the company, who would be the first to make contact with a school.) Most of the schools we went into were predominantly white, and the image which the children had of Black people was one which they'd received from television, and it was pretty negative. So I felt I couldn't take on any of the 'baddie' roles, for fear of reinforcing colour stereotyping. This was a great shame as I was dying to have a go at playing a 'baddie'!
>
> (unpublished interview, 1989)

Lorna raised an additional point for the Black female performer, which was the rare occurrence of 'colour-blind' casting. She was critical of Black performers being taken on on a colour basis, 'rather than on a we-want-this-person-in-our company basis'. Only once in her T.I.E. career had she experienced colour-blind casting which was when she was picked to play the part of Queen Victoria in a production 'not because Queen Victoria was white and I'm Black, but because I'm a woman and an actress capable of the part' (ibid.). Similarly, Elaine Grant and Jade Nanton, two of the three women in *Zerri's Choice* indicated in a brief interview held before their performance at Moat Community College, Leicester in 1989, that they were concerned to get away from the responsibility of carrying the colour banner. Their concern was again a professional one: good parts for good actresses.

These problems are raised not in order to be critical of the feminist groups who have placed race on their agenda, nor to take issue with the Black women performers who may take up critical positions within them, but to demonstrate the difficulties encountered as the white feminist theatre 'centre' is shaped by the Black 'margin'.

BLACK IDENTITIES AND BLACK COMPANIES

Whilst Black women who join white feminist companies bring the issue of race to a gender agenda, Black women who have come through a theatrical route which foregrounds race rather than feminism encounter a related, but different, set of problems. In contradistinction to the previous section, examples in this part detail work by Black women to come out of a Black theatrical context – possibly male, possibly female, possibly mixed – but above all Black. hooks details the links which Black women have with Black men in their fight against racism. Colour does not blind Black women to the sexism of the Black male, but they do share 'the experience of political solidarity' (hooks 1984: 69). This, in conjunction with understanding the racism of the Women's Movement itself, helps to explain why some Black women have chosen to prioritize race above gender in finding a route for their creativity, choosing a 'Black' artistic context for their work, rather than one based primarily on gender.

Yvonne Brewster

In 1987 Methuen published its first volume of *Black Plays*. A second volume followed in 1989. Both were introduced by the Black West

Indian director Yvonne Brewster. Brewster's introduction to the first volume indicates that the main impulse behind the collection is to bring together work which is finding a 'space' for the Black voice as part of British culture:

> This is the first anthology ever of plays written by and about black people living in Britain ...
>
> The book is more than timely when one considers the emphasis which the funding bodies have recently been placing on the cultural needs and the work of the black community. The work of those who live in this country must become more accessible; if not, then the work of playwrights living in the Caribbean and Africa will continue to dominate the scene as their plays are more readily available in the Educational editions meant for the schools of the Third World. These 'source' plays establish vital links with essential cultural roots, but the indigenous voice is just as important ...
>
> Living as part of a 'minority' in England whose artistic voice could become subsumed in the feverish maelstrom of theatrical activity, we have to ensure that we remain truly visible and audible. We can do this in our honest plays.
>
> (Brewster 1987: 7–8)

The politics of Black identity is seen as the common factor uniting the plays in both volumes. It is a dominant concern of Brewster's own work as a director with her company Talawa which she founded in the mid-1980s, and which now has a London building base: the Jeanetta Cochrane Theatre. In an interview for *New Theatre Quarterly* she identified the problematics of 'feminism' in relation to her movement between countries and cultures, which further underlines the primacy of racial as opposed to sexist oppression for Brewster as a West Indian woman:

> I came from a very strong West Indian background, and in the West Indies the word 'feminism' has a really hollow ring, simply because it's a matriarchal society. The women rule the roost without actually wearing the trousers. So, entering a European or British situation, one finds the feminist concept a bit difficult. It's hard to understand what all the fuss is about. But I suppose in a way that Talawa is exceedingly feminist, if to be feminist means to look at things from a feminist perspective or a female perspective.
>
> (Brewster 1991: 361)

At the time of the interview, however, Talawa, despite the way in which the company was 'slanted toward the female' (362), had not produced any woman-authored plays. Brewster explains this in relation to the company's working style which she identifies as 'epic', 'in the sense that we use big, bold powerful images' (362), as opposed to women's writing for theatre which she perceives as concerned with the 'small scale':

> we in Talawa need large sweeping epic plays, which might or might not deal with the domestic and the small-scale or private sides of life, but which must also look outward. Women are doing this in their lives, but not so much in their theatre.
>
> (363)

She states her interest in working 'historically and ritualistically' on plays that are 'political and apt and timely' (364–5), but is less concerned with feminism in its European context, which does not connect directly with her racial background. Like hooks, Brewster sees men as being part of the struggle for change:

> I suppose I feel that I'm a bit too old to take on the more radical aspects of feminism. But then that's not only because of my age, but also because of my origins, my background. And of course, I'm from a different generation than you young feminists today. We share a sense of the richness of women's contributions, but as far as I'm concerned, men don't have to be excluded from that. In fact, I think men can and (in my experience) often do help and encourage women's accomplishments, just as women encourage men and other women.
>
> (365)

That said, Brewster's own defining sense of Black women's theatre is that where possible it ought to be 'theatre written and directed and played by black women', or at the very least 'directed by black women' (368). This may account for some of the difficulties of 'white' groups with multi-cultural policies, where it is not always possible to have Black women in the key positions of writer, director, and designer. Further, it explains why other Black women who share Brewster's view of the need for artistic control of their material, their aesthetics, have created their own 'spaces'.

Jacqueline Rudet

The young Black British dramatist Jacqueline Rudet – who has a London East End and Dominican background – founded the company Imani-Faith (1983, now defunct) to produce work by and for Black women. The need for this was reinforced when Rudet experienced the Black male direction of her play *Money to Live*, professionally performed by the Black Theatre Co-operative at the Royal Court Theatre Upstairs, 1984. The Black Theatre Co-operative is a mixed company, founded in 1979 by Mustapha Matura and Charlie Hanson, with the aim of encouraging the work of Black practitioners and writers in British theatre. Rudet's experience of Hanson's direction of *Money to Live* was a less than happy one as it failed to understand the gender concerns in the play: a Black-woman-centred narrative which treats the issue of women stripping to get enough 'money to live':

> The production . . . could have been better. I didn't agree to the director. He actually made it hard for me to explain the play to the cast, contradicting me behind my back. It was a mistake having a man direct the play.
>
> In the production, he created a scene where Charlene and Judy perform at a club. Without my consent, he removed the scene where Charlene and Judy rehearse. This is an important scene. The girls take their clothes off, then they put them back on again. This scene shows how mechanical stripping becomes for a stripper; the play is not about stripping but the scene should not have been omitted. A man can't deal with the truth. What women create in life, men destroy.
>
> (Rudet 1986: 180; see also Chapter 7, p. 95)

Rudet did not make the same mistake with her play *Basin* (1985), the one woman-authored contribution in Methuen's first volume of *Black Plays*. *Basin* was directed by Paulette Randall, one of the founding members of the Theatre of Black Women, started in 1982. Randall's direction as a Black woman was essential to this piece which had moved on from the hard-times narrative of *Money to Live*, which in Rudet's view did not need to 'be treated as a 'black' play (Rudet 1986: 180), to a focus on the friendship between Black women in which Black identity was central to the friends, 'zammies' in the piece:

> The two 'zammies' in *Basin* become lovers but 'zammie' is

not 'lesbian' in patois. The word refers more to the universality of friendship between black women; no matter what nationality, no matter what class, all black women have very important things in common. They're the last in line; there's no one below them to oppress. Whether they like it or not, every black woman is the 'zammie' of every other black woman. It's almost an obligatory thing. As one of the girls in *Basin* says, 'Who will love us?'

(Rudet 1987: 114)

This bonding between Black women is important in their fight against oppression which helps them to define 'feminism' on their own terms.

Theatre of Black Women

This was very much the aim of the Black women's company the Theatre of Black Women founded by Bernardine Evaristo, Patricia Hilaire, and Paulette Randall. A *Spare Rib* review of their production *Silhouette* (1984) by a Black female reviewer makes this clear:

The stated objective of the Theatre of Black Women is to give artistic expression to the experience of Black women past and present. By reliving our history and current struggle in front of our eyes, these aims, I believe, will be instrumental in helping Black women to define and name our own brand of 'feminism', a noun which so far means little to me, appropriated as it has been to describe white women's experiences. This lack of definition and name for our long struggles has cost us dearly when trying to gain the cohesion necessary to demand our share of the power. This play may not have been perfect (what is?) but I can't knock anything which is trying to make Black women visible in roles other than those which have been foisted upon us.

('Maxine', *Spare Rib*, January 1984, 47)

The early work of the company was written by themselves. Their inaugural production in 1982 was a triple-bill of one-woman shows which shared the common theme of looking at the experience of being young, Black, and female in Britain: *Tiger Teeth Clenched Not to Bite* by Bernardine Evaristo, *Hey Brown Girl* by

Patricia Hilaire, and *Chameleon* by Paulette Randall. After *Silhouette* came *Pyeyucca* by Evaristo and Hilaire, again focusing on Black female identity in a white society.

In 1986 the company worked with the Scottish–Nigerian lesbian poet and dramatist Jackie Kay on her first play *Chiaroscuro*. The style of *Chiaroscuro* – worked out of music, dance, dialogue, and poetry – was influenced by Kay's own writing of poetry, and Shange's *For Colored Girls* which had impressed Kay by the way in which it was able to make 'poetry work as theatre' (Kay 1987: 83). Importantly, *Chiaroscuro* tackled not only the question of Black female identity, but like Rudet's *Basin*, also focused on the issue of sexuality:

> In all of the drafts of this play I have been obsessed with naming. What do we call ourselves as lesbians and black women? How did we get our names? How do we assert our names? What are our past names? Each of the characters tells the story of her name. She is also searching for another name. She is in flux, reassessing her identity, travelling back into memory and forward into possibility. In order to change we have to examine who we say we are and how much of that has been imposed.
>
> (Kay 1987: 82)

The company diversified its material in 1987, producing the acclaimed one-woman show *The Cripple* by Ruth Harris, based on the true, moving story of a Jamaican woman crippled from birth overcoming her disability; a piece of children's theatre, *Miss Quashi and the Tiger's Tail* by Gabriela and Jean Pearse; and a second play by Harris, *The Children*. However, the company could not survive the hard financial times, and like several other small companies in the 1980s, disbanded in 1988.

CLAIMING A 'SPACE': BLACK WOMEN PERFORMANCE POETS

The financial squeeze on companies has increasingly reduced the avenues and outlets available for Black women's work. Although Brewster argued at the end of the 1980s that the 'Black voice' in Britain was gaining strength (1989: ix), the 1990s seem to be silencing its rhythms, or at least as far as Black women's theatre is concerned.

That said, one 'space' Black women have claimed is through the work of performance poets, rooted in the oral traditions of the African, Afro-Caribbean storytelling. The Afro-Caribbean performance poet, Amryl Johnson, for instance, who was born in Trinidad but brought up in England from the age of eleven, talks, sings, and recites in English and Creole (a selection of her poems and prose is available as a taped anthology: *Blood and Wine*). Through this medium she is able to explore her double exile: that of 'her people as slaves from their native Africa as the first exile' and 'her own removal to England' as a second exile (press release for *Blood and Wine*, Cofa Press: 1991).

Performance poetry is sometimes also rooted in more fully theatricalized performance contexts. Performance poet Jean 'Binta' Breeze performed Shange's *The Love Space Demands* in October 1992. It was the first woman-authored production by Talawa, and fulfilled Brewster's sense of 'epic' by synthesizing the Shange poems and monologues performed by 'Binta' Breeze with music and choreographed movement. Similarly, Grace Nichols's poetry is the 'source' text for the performing arts video text *i is a long memoried woman*, which fuses the oral traditions of the poetry and the speaking voice of the poet, with narration, dance, movement, music, etc. (see Chapter 10).

Drawing on the traditions of orality is a way of linking with the culture of the Black diaspora, important to the identity politics of Black women in Britain. As Parmar explains:

> In these post-modernist times the question of identity has taken on colossal weight particularly for those of us who are post-colonial migrants inhabiting histories of diaspora. Being cast into the role of the Other, marginalized, discriminated against, and too often invisible, not only within everyday discourses of affirmation but also within the 'grand narratives' of European thought, black women in particular have fought to assert privately and publicly our sense of self: a self that is rooted in particular histories, cultures and languages.
>
> (1989: 58)

Performance poetry represents a way of challenging the Eurocentric 'grand narratives' of the stage, and for the Black female spectator offers an affirmation of her 'sense of self', by making visible the 'colonial landscape' of a culture and history she carries with her.

7

PERFORMING GENDER
A materialist practice

GENDER THEORY

During the 1980s theorizing gender became the centre of a 'new phase' of critical study. Some feminists are concerned that a shift in focus from feminist studies to gender studies might result in a 'phase-out' of the former, particularly if marginalized by the growing field of cultural study concerned with masculinity (for an overview of discussion on this point see Modelski 1991: 4–6). However, from another feminist viewpoint 'gender trouble' is seen as the evolution of feminist enquiry in which the first phase of accepting the 'presumed universality and unity of the subject of feminism' is now subjected to questioning (Butler 1990: 4). As Judith Butler argues, 'the premature insistence on a stable subject of feminism, understood as a seamless category of women, inevitably generates multiple refusals to accept the category' (ibid.).

The previous chapter on Black women's theatre is evidence of the kind of refusal to which Butler refers. De Lauretis (1987) in fact attributes the 'shift in feminist consciousness' during the 1980s to the publication in 1981 of an anthology of writings by 'radical women of color' (*This Bridge Called My Back*, edited by C. Moraga and G. Anzaldua). The 'shift' De Lauretis argues:

> is best characterized by the awareness and the effort to work through feminism's complicity with ideology, both ideology in general (including classism, or bourgeois liberalism, racism, colonialism, imperialism, and, I would also add, with some qualifications, humanism) and the ideology of gender in particular – that is to say, heterosexism.
>
> (10–11)

This final chapter before the case studies complements previous discussion and documentation of the class-based, colour-based challenges to feminism, by focusing specifically on the ways in which gender is troubling the theory and practice of feminist theatre/s. It surveys the theory and practice of gender critiques; the training and workshop methods which enable women to 'know' how their bodies are constructed in the representational frame of 'Woman'; and looks specifically at the ways in which the theory and practice of lesbian theatre challenges gender.

ALIENATING GENDER

The feminist practice of theatre based on the Brechtian model (as discussed in Chapter 5), has more recently received critical attention by feminists investigating its deconstructive potential in the field of gender representation. In her influential essay 'Brechtian Theory/Feminist Theory: Toward a Gestic Feminist Criticism' Elin Diamond argues persuasively that the Brechtian/feminist model offers a means of 'dismantling the gaze' (1988: 83). She argues that where feminist film theory has occupied itself with a critique of the gaze, feminist theatre studies has something of its own to offer: 'we, through Brechtian theory, have something to give them: a female body in representation that resists fetishization and a viable position for the female spectator' (ibid.). Diamond surveys key elements of Brechtian theory (the A-effect, the alienated 'not but' style of acting, historicization, and *Gestus*) in relation to a key concern of feminism: the 'analysis of gender in material social relations and in discursive and representational structures' (82–3). Through her analysis Diamond is able to demonstrate the potential of a feminist/Brechtian *Gestus* for removing the sight/site of the female body out of its objectified position in the 'male gaze' to a site/sight of 'looking-at-being-looked-at-ness' (84–9). More specifically Diamond states:

> If feminist theory sees the body as culturally mapped and gendered, Brechtian historicization insists that this body is not a fixed essence but a site of struggle and change. If feminist theory is concerned with the multiple and complex signs of a woman's life: her color, her age, her desires, her politics – what I want to call her *historicity* – Brechtian theory gives us a way to put that historicity on view – in the theatre.

In its conventional iconicity, theatre laminates body to character, but the body in historicization stands visibly and palpably separate from the 'role' of the actor as well as the role of the character; it is always insufficient and open.

(89)

Jill Dolan's chapter on materialist-feminist performance, influenced by Diamond's essay, summarizes the types of Brechtian-based, critical distancing techniques which have been used in a range of American feminist productions to intervene in the gaze (1988: 99–117). These include the disruption of realist conventions of performing and staging, casting women against convention (i.e. gendered stereotypes), or the use of puppets and dolls to create a *Gestus* which critically examines gendered relations. One key alienating-gender technique in feminist performance, which will provide the illustration for discussion in this section, is the construction of the female body as a site/sight of 'looking-at-being-looked-at-ness' in performance, through playing with the vestimentary codes of gendered costume in relation to the body. This may be en-acted in three main ways: the costumed body is over-displayed, under-displayed, or cross-displayed.

Over-display

In the instance of over-display, 'lookingness' is effected by alienating the vestimentary sign-system of the 'feminine'. This is the case, for example, in some feminist experimentation with the cabaret form. In *Floorshow* (1977/8) and *Time Gentlemen Please* (1978), Monstrous Regiment created the opportunities for generating a critical discourse surrounding the subservient, decorative role which the form traditionally requires women to en-act. By deconstructing the objectification of women in this context, the company moved towards the 'looking-at-being-looked-at-ness' and the body as a site of *historicity* which Diamond describes. The problematics of this, however, were highlighted in the case of *Time Gentlemen Please* where attempts to foreground the construction of femininity through the deconstructive use of 'feminine' costuming was misread. One performance of this piece ended in an angry riot, as feminist spectators did not read the foregrounding of the costuming as a gendered sign-system, or read the traces of the repressed in the 'not but' representation of female sexuality (see Hanna 1991: xlii–xliii).

The British cabaret trio Fascinating Aïda established a group identity in the 1980s by parodying the dominant stereotype of the glamorous woman: 'their appeal was broad, their message was ballsy, but their dresses were low-cut and slinky' (Emma Freud, Radio 4 interview with the trio, 1992). Their alienation of glamour dress codes, encoded in the appearance of the performers and the parodic lyrics of their songs, was summed up in their farewell concert in 1989: 'A Farewell to Sequins'. The parody was topical for the 1980s given the power-dressing glamour of the American soaps, and the 'Superwoman' image which women on both sides of the Atlantic were supposed to live up to.

The 'over-display' technique also appears in feminist drama. In Rudet's *Money to Live*, discussed in Chapter 6, there is a scene in which the stripper Judy instructs Charlene how to strip:

> *Charlene's room, one early evening. Pulsating, sensual dance music plays, while a strobe light flashes on and off. Judy is teaching Charlene a few moves. Both wear typical costumes. Judy is instructing the sexiest way to uncover breasts. Judy demonstrates. Charlene attempts, Judy motions that it's not right. Charlene puts her top piece back on and tries again. Judy motions that she's got it right this time.*

> (1986: 165)

This scene shows the female body being constructed as an image for male consumption. The emphasis on 'over-display', on rehearsing/constructing the female body as a spectacle, transforms the body from a sight of looking to 'lookingness'. This further underlines Rudet's anger at the male director's decision to cut the scene and replace it with a striptease club scene: a woman as object-on-display-scene (see Chapter 6, p. 88).

Under-display

Techniques which alienate the representation of gender by constructing the female body as a sight of 'under-display' constitute a reversal of the first technique: in performance contexts which construct the expectation of the female body on display, the body is instead hidden. For example, the Chuffinelles, another British cabaret company, work in the opposite way to Fascinating Aïda: they parody the glamour of cabaret by performing as a trio of apparently non-glamorous older women, costumed in loose clothing which does not emphasize the body, but conceals it. The Chuffs self-referentially draw the audience's attention to the dislocation of glamour-expectation in the course of performing. Feminist theatre which foregrounds male-authored violence against the female body (see Chapter 9) employs a variety of techniques which work to under-display the body. In dominant cultural forms, the victimization of the body is re-enacted for the male gaze, as demonstrated, for example, in the flashback sequence of the multiple-rape scene in the 1980s mainstream cinematic text, *The Accused*. By contrast, Franca Rame's one-woman piece *The Rape* critically distances the rape commentary from the performer's body (in Hood 1991 [1975]). The spectator is not allowed to 'see' the body displayed as victim/object, but is forced into a position which requires her/him to confront the issue of male violence (see also *Ficky Stingers* by Eve Lewis, in Remnant 1987). *Tissue* by Louise Page which dramatizes the subject of breast cancer and mastectomy, keeps the body concealed in order to critique the concept of the perfect female body image, and to avoid representing Sally (the patient) as a disfigured object of curiosity. Page explains:

> Elizabeth [Revil], consistent in the role of Sally, had a dress. It was a sort of mauve pink. A smock type dress which she could wear as a nightie, little girl's dress and a going out dress. I didn't want Sally ever to be seen naked. It was important that the audience knew she carried the trauma of mastectomy but that it was unseen.
>
> (Page 1982: 101)

Page's Brechtian-styled, reported montage of scenes does not draw the spectator into the 'story' of a victim, but instructs and educates her/him to take action.

Cross-gendered display

Techniques of cross-gendered costume display also require the hiding of the female body. Such techniques constitute a dominant method of 'troubling gender' in contemporary feminist theatrical practice. Churchill's *Cloud Nine* is one of the most frequently cited examples of a cross-dressing gender critique, as is Benmussa's theatricalization of the 'perhapser' Albert Nobbs in an adaptation of George Moore's short story *The Singular Life of Albert Nobbs*

(Benmussa: 1979). Albert Nobbs is the narrative of a woman who disguises herself as a man in order to earn a better wage. Benmussa explains the importance of costuming in relation to the male disguise:

> Her costume must be strict and plain, black and white. She is imprisoned in this costume, which is at the same time armour, yoke and defence. Her costume has become her body. This was the starting point from which I directed the actresses. Nobb's shoes are important too: big, men's shoes which anchor her to the ground, give her weight. I had to expose the scandal that a woman's body hidden under this man's body represents for society.
>
> (Benmussa 1979: 22)

On the other hand, Benmussa had the female body made visible via its displaced representation in the maidservants: 'the woman in her transpires, emerges, is "represented" behind her, beside her, around her, as the maidservants, going about their work, make feminine gestures' (25).

A more recent example of a cross-dressing narrative of transgression is Dorothy Talk's production of *Walking on Peas* by Erika Block. Material for the play was derived from the military histories of female cross-dressers (see Wheelwright 1989). The play's cross-dressing narratives follow the fortunes and desires of Isabe Bunken/Isaiah Bunk and Princess Kati Dadeshkeliani/Prince Djamal who are both 'walking on peas'. (Dorothy Talk's production publicity explicates the 'walking on peas' concept with a quotation from Decker and Van de Pol's *The Tradition of Female Transvestism in Early Modern Europe* as follows: 'Tricks to determine whether one is dealing with a woman: . . . scatter peas on the ground: the man has a firm step, the woman falls.') It is not a 'singular' life which is staged, but a community of 'singular lives', and one, moreover, which mirrors the dangers of disguise and desire experienced by lesbian communities (see last section of this chapter for further discussion).

Off-stage it is also possible to see how a young generation of women is currently making use of gender-encoded 'costume' in their everyday lives by mixing the vestimentary codes assigned to the 'masculine' and the 'feminine'. By wearing outfits which combine Doc Marten boots with floral skirts, or a man's dinner jacket with brightly coloured leggings, young women are making use of their dress codes to signal their own 'not but' critique of gender representation. Julia Macpherson, interviewed by *Feminist Review* as a 'younger feminist' in their charting of feminism over the past twenty years, for example, stated that she hoped that her use of contrasting masculine/feminine styles ('mini-skirt with Doctor Martens') neither reinforced the feminine nor clashed with her feminism, but instead was read as an expression of her young feminist position and outlook at the end of the 1980s (interview, 1989: 139).

WORKSHOPPING GENDER

De Lauretis explains the contradictory experience for women in being represented as 'Woman', whilst knowing 'as feminists' that they 'are not *that*' (1987: 10). As the opening section of this chapter has shown, feminist theatre constructs 'spaces' in which it is possible to confront and explore that contradiction. In order for there to be a sustained theorized theatrical practice with regard to gender, women require performance training methods which will enable them to en-act the 'not *that*' critique. The feminist theatre workshop is, therefore, an important laboratory space for investigating the processes of 'performing gender', as this section aims to show.

In 'Poetics of the Oppressed' the Brazilian theatre director Augusto Boal proposes that the first stage of transforming a spectator into an actor is 'knowing the body', and in relation to this process suggests that 'there is a great number of exercises designed with the objective of making each person aware of his own body, of his bodily possibilities, and of deformations suffered because of the type of work he performs' (1979: 127). Boal's 'exercises of this first stage are designed to "undo" the muscular structure of the participants' in order that each participant can then feel 'to what point his body is governed by his work' (128). Boal's 'Poetics of the Oppressed' is, however, expressed in terms of social class, not gender, and overlooks the fact that 'knowing the body' is very different for the female performer and the socialization of her body which 'governs' its movement. It is, however, important if the female performer is to know her body in order to be able to control it, that she begins with examining the poetics of gender oppression which deform it.

Unfortunately, many of the introductory workshop techniques

used in practical theatre courses assume a (masculine) norm. This point was recently raised and debated in a workshop on 'Gender Issues in Drama/Theatre Departments' led by Gerry Harris at the annual British conference of the Standing Committee for University Drama Departments (Lancaster: March 1993). On gender issues in the workshop Harris cited the number of ways in which female students are 'abused' by theatre training exercises. For example, a number of trust exercises involve a participant 'trusting' their bodies to be caught by other members of the group. Such exercises do not, however, as Harris indicated, take account of the ways in which women are socialized into feeling uncomfortable about their body size and weight – specifically the anxiety around letting other people know how much they weigh. Yet women are constrained by the workshop forum to participate in exercises under the same conditions as their male counterparts. Such exercises serve only to keep the female participant from 'knowing her body', and to reinforce her anxieties about her body in its socially constructed 'feminine' context.

That said, in a *supportive* workshop environment the female participant can learn to know how her body is deformed by the gender sign-system 'Woman' in exercises based on movement activities which she is socially conditioned into avoiding: ball games, running, etc. Jill Greenhalgh offers a training exercise which is based on circles of stick throwing. Participants are arranged in a small circle and are taken through a series of exercises which begin with a simple passing of sticks around the edge of the circle, to the random passing of sticks across the circle, to the breaking up of the circle and participants being able to throw the sticks on the move. In mixed groups, the difference between male and female participants is usually immediately apparent. It is generally the case that the male has been socialized, mainly through exposure to sporting activities, into an aptitude for throwing and catching. The female participant's initial reactions tend to be fearful of catching the stick, self-defensive, apologetic if she mis-throws, etc.

Yet, ultimately, women have more to gain from this exercise because it engages them in a series of movements which free-up the body, contrary to the way in which they have been 'instructed' to be restrained, constrained by experience of their engendered socialization. The experience of the female participant may, therefore, be one of empowerment. Elsewhere, Dolan has argued that 'a feminist acting technique has to embody physical and emotional strength' (1984: 11). Greenhalgh's exercise offers female participants a training technique which develops the physical co-ordination required to create 'presence', makes her aware of the ways in which she is, in everyday terms, physically encouraged to be 'weak', and allows her to 'know' the strengths of her own body.

As previously stated, Cristina Castrillo's actor training method based on physical and emotional memories, is one which enables the performer to workshop and perform personal material without endangering the performer. Many of Castrillo's training exercises are useful to women because they, like Greenhalgh's stick exercise, encourage physical strength and control, which, socially, a woman is conditioned into believing she cannot achieve. Many of the exercises can also be taken as departure points for creative work. The mirror exercise which was outlined in Chapter 5 (see p. 72), for example, may be developed in a workshop context into a laboratory-based exploration of 'refusing the gaze'. Seeing the body at the mirror reawakens the performer's experience of the fictional construct of the Woman who is looked at, but the experience is isolated in a way in which the performer, through her body, also speaks: 'But I am not that.'

Training and knowing the body are important and related aspects of developing an awareness of gender and gesture. Hilary Ramsden and Jude Winter, who were formerly members of Siren (see later under 'lesbian theatre') and who now form the company Dorothy Talk, offer mixed and women-only workshops in both America and Britain, with a focus on gesture. In particular, the women-only workshop environment is a space which enables women to become aware of the ways in which they are imaged through gesture, and, importantly, how, through gesture, they may intervene in the image-making. For example, one exercise involves working in pairs to create a series of gestures of affection repeated as a sequence which is offered by one woman to another. The women discover how meaning is encoded in their gestures by changing the proxemic relations of the performer, by experimenting with pace, facial expression or the absence of expression, changing eye contact, etc. Working in female pairs changes the dominant economy of gestural exchanges of affection between men and women. In this way, the exercise encourages women to find gestural traces of that which is not represented, and, if workshopped further, could provide a departure point for creating a representational frame based on an economy of female desire and subjectivity.

Similarly, Monique Wittig and Sande Zeig in America have worked in a workshop context to look at how gestures produce meaning, and, more specifically, to examine the possibilities of deconstructing gender through gesture. Zeig's description of this work points to the way in which 'gestures are material, as material as clothing which one may "put on" and "take off"' (1985: 13). Their workshop programme was designed to reawaken the ways in which 'playing the woman' and 'playing the man' are socially constructed, by directing exercises 'toward finding one's "impersonator"; that is, the person one would be if one were of the opposite sex' (14). Through such a process the participant is able to 'put on' and 'take off' languages of masculine and feminine gesture. Zeig explains that this is important in the fight against oppression. To move within the framework of feminine gesture is to demonstrate 'that one is in agreement with and accepts a system that has literally made more than half of the population infirm' (13). Zeig continues 'if we as lesbians are fighting oppression, we cannot reproduce the gestures assigned to the class of women, because the gestures designated to the class of women are the gestures of slaves' (13).

Zeig points out that the workshopping of gender and gesture was designed for the 'social actor', but indicates its importance for work in the theatre. All of the workshop methods described in this section work from a similar base-line: they too may be used to defamiliarize the ways in which women play Woman in their everyday lives, as well as being used for actor training programmes.

LESBIAN THEATRE

Deconstructing gender is, as Zeig describes, an area of central concern to lesbians seeking to intervene in contemporary theatre practice. The 'trouble with gender' centrally informs the communities of lesbian theatre whose practice has much to offer the current theoretical field of gender studies and feminist theatre practice/s.

Finding a 'space' for exploring lesbian criticism and performance has been difficult to achieve in both America and Britain. The previous chapter demonstrated how the Liberation Movement in its formative years insisted on women as the same rather than different. This generally meant that the lesbian position was overlooked, or if she was allowed an appearance it was always as 'a bridesmaid and never the bride'(Case 1989b: 284). The position in theatre was similar. Creating a space for women to explore their theatrical creativity, usually in the form of setting up a group, would generally elide the possibility of there being a space for lesbian theatre. Writing the introduction for Methuen's first volume of *Lesbian Plays*, the editor Jill Davis comments that:

> only two plays in our 'sister' series *Plays By Women* are on lesbian subjects. This is not intended as a criticism of the editors of that series; their choice accurately represents the extent of inclusion of lesbians within the mainstream of women's theatre writing.
>
> (1987: 9)

The lesbian subject on and off the stage offers the possibility of a radical challenge to the dominant representations of gender, because she has no investment in a gender economy based on sexual difference:

> The lesbian subject is in a position to denaturalize dominant codes by signifying an existence that belies the entire structure of heterosexual culture and its representations . . . The lesbian is a refusor of culturally imposed gender ideology, who confounds representation based on sexual difference and on compulsory heterosexuality.
>
> (Dolan 1988: 116)

It follows that in lesbian performance the 'lesbian desire underlying lesbian representations of gender disrupts the system of gender signification' (Dolan: 116); it is a means of foregrounding representation in the lesbian style of 'not but' practice.

One technique central to a lesbian practice of gender alienation is the butch–femme couple, whose deconstructive potential is most persuasively argued for by Case in her essay 'Toward a Butch–Femme Aesthetic' (1989b). She explains that 'the butch–femme couple inhabit the subject position together' (283), that together they make one, and together they critique the fictions of gender in a way which empowers them with the agency to move outside of ideology rather than remain entrapped within its structures:

> From a theatrical point of view, the butch–femme roles take on the quality of something more like a character construction . . . Thus, these roles qua roles lend agency and self-determination to the historically passive subject, providing her with at least two options for gender identification and with the aid of camp, an irony that allows her perception to be constructed from outside ideology, with a gender role that makes her appear as if she is inside of it.
>
> (292)

Case's argument is informed by the work of the American lesbian company Split Britches, and in particular by the company's on- and off-stage butch–femme couple, Lois Weaver and Peggy Shaw (for details see Case 1989b: 294–7). Split Britches came out of the WOW cafe (Women's One World), a lesbian performance space on the Lower East Side of New York, which began life as a cafe in 1980 (for details of the inception and evolution of WOW cafe see Solomon 1985). The use of the butch–femme couple is central to their lesbian performance style, as it enables them to playfully put on and take off the gendered sign-systems of appearance. Role swapping, moving in and out of narratives, the couple play with the structures of representation, without being contained within them, as would be the case in the restricted narrative space of a realistic framework (see Case 1989b: 297).

Central to this kind of gender-play is the use of popular culture (see Dolan 1985b). By critiquing popular genres lesbian performers are able to alienate generically engendered stereotyping. Siren has worked extensively in this way. The group's biggest success, *Pulp* (1985/6), by company member Tasha Fairbanks who has scripted most of the group's material over the years, plays with the conventions and style of the 1950s film noir in a celebration of lesbian desire and glamour. Playing with and through popular cultural forms in this way mirrors the position of the lesbian subject as outsider in relation to dominant culture, but also offers her a way of encoding, inscribing, and subverting them with her own desires. Company members Jane Boston and Jude Winter explained in interview how important it was in terms of the group's history to find ways of moving away from a first phase of investigating the oppressive systems of a male-dominated world, to finding a way, as they did in *Pulp*, of performing and celebrating their own identity and culture as lesbians:

Jane Boston: *Pulp* was very much an attempt to look at what we are: let's turn to our culture, to lesbianism in particular, let's look at something celebratory, let's look at something exotic, let's look at sexuality.

Jude Winter: So we changed in two ways. One related to content: we decided to look at not making statements about why women should be lesbians – everybody in the company was lesbian anyway so we saw no point in even discussing that – but at different lesbian roles like the bad lady, the vamp, etc., so that there was a change in emphasis. The second way in which we changed related to style. We decided to look at the genre of the 1950s movies so we had a lot of stylistic elements to explore. We went – for the first time – for glamour. We had said it was time that lesbian theatre hit out with glamorous women.

(unpublished interview, Siren Theatre, 1989)

In such a performance context the lesbian spectator is offered a lesbian subject. The gaze is not 'male' or 'female' but lesbian:

When the lesbian performer uses her desire for other lesbians as the driving force in her work, her representation of herself for others like herself becomes a model played out in time, with people, and in space of a self-sufficient system that drops the male subject and sexual difference from the address.

(Davy 1986: 48)

As Dolan argues: 'lesbians are appropriating the subject position of the male gaze by beginning to articulate the exchange of desire between women. Lesbian subjectivity creates a new economy of desire' (1989b: 64).

An understanding of the 'new economy of desire' created between lesbian spectator and lesbian subject was reinforced in the specific instance of a recent gay production where the exchange of desire between women was overshadowed by the gay male gaze. *Belle Reprieve*, which played with the fictional constructs of narrative, character, and, most importantly, desire, in Tennesse Williams's *A Street Car Named Desire*, was a co-production between the gay company Bloolips and Split Britches which was touring Britain in 1992. The co-production played at the Phoenix Theatre, Leicester (an alternative arts centre venue) to a mixed theatre audience, but one which consisted in the main of gay men. In this performance context the play between Weaver and Shaw risked being upstaged and marginalized by the dominant gaze which passed between Bloolips and the gay (male) spectator: in particular, the economy of desire constructed through the 'glamour' of the male drag performance. Although the play between the pairings – Weaver as Stella and Shaw as Stanley, and Precious Pearl as Mitch and Bette Bourne as Blanche – challenged and de-stabilized the 'fixing' of gender within a heterosexual framework, there were dangers surrounding the imagery of Woman in the Bourne/Blanche drag performance. On the issue of gay male drag, Dolan observes that:

> Women fare no better. Female impersonation here is usually filtered through the camp sensibility, which removes it from the realm of serious gender play and deconstruction ... both spectator and performer conspire to construct a male-identified subject that is left out of the terms of exchange: women are non-existent in drag performance, but woman-as-myth, as a cultural, ideological object, is constructed in an agreed exchange between the male performer and the usually male spectator. Male drag mirrors women's socially constructed roles.
>
> (1985a: 8)

Moreover, Dolan points out that in the 'gender game' of gay male drag, gay men can 'easily assume female roles, knowing that offstage, they wear the clothes of the social elite', whereas 'the situation for women and lesbians is much more precarious' (ibid.). Perhaps, in a co-produced gay and lesbian piece like *Belle Reprieve*, deconstructive gender play needs to take more account of this. (A very different play of gender and desire for lesbian/women spectators would have arisen, for example, if Weaver had been assigned the lesbian-femme playing of Blanche.)

The question of what happens to the lesbian gaze in performance contexts in which the spectating community is not restricted to lesbian membership is a very vexing one for lesbian theorists and critics. Schneider's interview with Holly Hughes (1989a), author of *Dress Suits to Hire* performed by Shaw and Weaver, raises this issue (the script of *Dress Suits to Hire* is published with the interview: see Hughes 1989b). In the interview, Schneider asks Hughes for an opinion on the view put forward by Case on the performance of *Dress Suits* at Michigan University, Ann Arbor: that the piece ought to be performed in a woman-only context and that the university-audience context undermined its radicalism. Hughes, however, had a different view to offer, which was that the lesbian position was one which different kinds of people could relate to:

> I really believe in art and I believe in allowing the audience to have their own personal subjective view. I give the audience a lot of credit – I think people are really bored with a straight white male perspective in theatre and can relate to the story in a lot of ways. A lot of people have experienced being an outsider. Everybody feels queer in some sense of the word. I think that there are various windows into an experience . . . all of a sudden they're inside of an experience that's formed by a lesbian.
>
> (Hughes, in interview, 1989a: 176)

The changing role of the spectator in the production of meaning in lesbian theatre which stays in the margins and lesbian theatre which moves into the mainstream remains an issue for debate (see Davy 1989: 167). Furthermore, Dolan begins to speculate on the need 'not to reify the lesbian spectator as some new, unbroken, unified idol', and proposes the notion of thinking in terms of 'lesbian spectatorial communities', which would take account of class, race, and ideology (1989b: 64–5). 'As de Lauretis chastises', states Dolan:

> changing the shape of desire from heterosexual to lesbian won't get the entire crisis of representation off our backs. There is no universal lesbian spectator to whom each lesbian representation will provide the embodiment of the same lesbian desire. Sexuality, and desire, and lesbian subjects are more complicated than that.
>
> (65)

Nevertheless, in terms of current investigations into representational activity, lesbian theatrical practice and the economy of its gaze has much to offer other feminist communities of women 'performing gender', all of whom are 'walking on peas'.

Part II

CASE STUDIES

8

THE 'PRISONHOUSE OF CRITICISM'

Susan Glaspell

THE 'LOST' DRAMATIST

Despite the controversy which Ibsen initially aroused in his contemporary critics, his position as a pioneer of the 'new drama', and his canonical status as the 'father' of modern drama have now been assured. Like Ibsen, the American playwright Susan Glaspell was also a turn-of-the-century pioneer of the 'new drama'. However, Glaspell's 'contemporary reputation as one of the two most accomplished playwrights of twentieth-century America may come as a legitimate surprise even to serious students of dramatic history' (Dymkowski 1988: 91). Unlike Ibsen, the American 'new dramatist' has been allowed to 'disappear'. That her 'disappearance' is rooted in the gender bias of the 'canon' is the central argument of this first case study which aims to pursue in detail some of the general observations and criticisms raised in Chapter 2. By examining the (male) reviewing of Glaspell's work, the study will show how gender bias contributed to the marginalization of Glaspell's theatre, which has only recently been reclaimed by feminist theatre historians. Given the obscurity into which Glaspell has fallen, this 'lost' dramatist needs a brief contextualizing introduction.

After an early career in journalism and writing Glaspell's work in the theatre began when she, along with her husband George Cram Cook, co-founded the Provincetown Players in the summer of 1915 at Provincetown, Massachusetts. The players were not professionals but were drawn from a community of intellectuals. Their first summer performances took place in a converted fishing shack which they named the 'Wharf Theatre' and in the ensuing winter months the company opened in premises on Macdougal Street, New York, which they christened the Playwrights' Theatre.

In 1918 the company moved to a larger building on Macdougal Street: the Provincetown Playhouse. Glaspell, who worked with the company until 1922, was central to the work in all three venues. During this period she authored four full-length plays, and seven one-act plays (two of which were co-authored with Cook). She also involved herself in aspects of staging, particularly acting and directing. In 1922 she and Cook left to live in Greece. Cook died in 1924, and Glaspell returned to America where her work included a further two full-length plays (one co-authored with her second husband, Norman Matson), and six more novels (she had already authored four) before her death in 1948 (for details of the plays see Waterman 1966: 66–91; Dymkowski 1988).

The Provincetown Players were recognized in their time as a pioneering force in the 'new' American drama, and, moreover, were credited with providing the platform for the two acknowledged new forces in American theatre: Susan Glaspell and Eugene O'Neill. Yet although theatre criticism during Glaspell's lifetime acknowledged (to a certain degree) her contribution to the 'new drama' alongside O'Neill's, it also constituted the first stage of its disappearance from the canon. This process can be examined in the commentary of the critic Ludwig Lewisohn.

As a critic, Lewisohn was generally supportive of Glaspell's work. On reviewing the first collected edition of Glaspell's plays, published in 1920, Lewisohn cites the low production values of the Provincetown Players as a reason why Glaspell's work had not received all the critical attention it deserved. As evidence he refers to the Washington Square Players (an experimental company founded in 1914 whose main aim was to explore European drama on the American stage, and which later became the Theatre Guild), whose production of Glaspell's one-act play *Trifles* he claimed 'gave a wide repute to what is by no means her best work' (Lewisohn 1920: 509). By contrast, he states that Glaspell's full-length play *Bernice*, 'not only her masterpiece but one of the indisputably important dramas of the modern English or American theater', was presented by 'the Provincetown Players with more than their accustomed feebleness and lack of artistic lucidity'. He concludes: 'The publication of Miss Glaspell's collected plays at last lifts them out of the tawdriness of their original production and lets them live by their own inherent life' (ibid.).

Lewisohn's reason for the overlooking of Glaspell's work is intriguing but inaccurate. While the performance of *Trifles* by the

Washington Square Players was certainly acknowledged as an example of 'conspicuously good acting' (Broun, *Tribune*, 14 November 1916, p.7), Lewisohn's claim for the poor acting of the Provincetown Players is refuted by the way in which it was customary for many of the players to perform in both companies (see Deutsch and Hanau 1931: 51), and by the increasing professionalism of the Provincetown Players between 1915 and 1920 (ibid.: 62). Furthermore, Glaspell herself played the key role of the servant Abbie in *Bernice* and her skills as an actress were generally highly rated. (Critics frequently cite Jacques Copeau on this point. Copeau saw Glaspell understudy for Ann Harding in *The Inheritors* (1921) which prompted him to pronounce her 'a truly great actress' (quoted in Deutsch and Hanau 1931: 25)).

The key to Glaspell's obscurity lies in Lewisohn's review itself. Lewisohn pens a portrait of Glaspell in the review as 'never quite spontaneous and unconscious and free, never the unquestioning servant of her art. She broods and tortures herself and weighs the issues of expression' (1920: 510). This is then set against what he describes as a surprising phenomenon: 'that four of her seven one-act plays are comedies'. He is able to account for this, however, by citing that two of them were in fact co-authored with Cook, her husband – someone possessed of 'a far less scrupulous and more ungirdled mind' (ibid.). Although Glaspell and Cook were the co-founders of the Provincetown Players, and occasional co-authors of one-act pieces, the foregrounding of Cook's contribution in both contexts at best detracts from and at worst eclipses Glaspell's own contribution to these two spheres of theatrical activity. As Mary Heaton Vorse (owner of the 'Wharf Theatre') later commented:

> A great deal of emphasis has always been put, and rightly, on George Cram Cook as the moving power which gave the impetus to the group and which made 'The Provincetown' the remarkable theater it was.
>
> Not enough has been said about Susan Glaspell and her quality of enthusiasm when a new idea absorbed her . . . Nor without her would George Cram Cook's intensive work in the theater have been possible. Her constant encouragement and her humor as well as her irony were the things which nourished him and made his never ending tasks possible.
>
> (1991 [1942]: 124)

In Lewisohn's later full-length study on American theatre he states that 'Susan Glaspell . . . definitely belongs to the period of the beginnings of the American theater' and sees in her theatre 'all the qualities and trends of those early years' (1932: 393). But, at the close of the section devoted to an overview of Glaspell's theatre, Lewisohn also makes a statement which effectively writes Glaspell out of the twentieth-century canon of 'greats':

> Miss Glaspell had enough metaphysical stamina and disdain of success to produce a small but coherent body of dramatic work. The new stages and the new playwrights plowed up the soil of art and of life and changed the spiritual scene of America. But of all their activity only fragments remain, brilliant but barren fragments, save for the work, with all its shortcomings, of one man, of Eugene O'Neill.
>
> (401)

If it was Cook who overshadowed Glaspell's contribution to the Provincetown Players as a theatrical enterprise, it was Eugene O'Neill's 'status' as playwright which overshadowed her as a dramatist. The two can be seen working in tandem in the following editorial introduction to O'Neill's plays in 1960:

> It was to the Provincetown Players under George Cram Cook that he owed his first productions. Most of his plays until the middle twenties had their first showing in Greenwich Village under Cook. Since then, he has come to occupy a position in America not unlike that of G.B.S. in England: the young rebel has become the Old Master.
>
> (Browne 1960: 8)

Like Ibsen, O'Neill's canonical upgrading from 'young rebel' to 'Old Master' is confirmed. Cook receives all the credit for the Provincetown Players. Glaspell receives no mention at all. Whereas O'Neill's plays were collected and anthologized by major publishing houses, Glaspell's were allowed to go out of print until Cambridge Press reprinted a selection of her plays in 1987 (edited by C. W. E. Bigsby).

WOMAN DRAMATIST AS PROFESSIONAL WRITER

What is frequently cited by Glaspell's contemporary critics is her inability to sustain a linear career pattern in the theatre. Quinn, for example, dismisses the theatre of Susan Glaspell and her contemporary Zona Gale in an argument which presents the two women dramatists as part-timers. It is implied that their work does not mature and progress to heights of 'greatness'. Of Gale and of Glaspell he writes, 'keen as their love for the theatre may be' they 'are more experimental than systematic in their work for it. This is shown clearly when we contrast their achievement with the plays of an expert craftsman, who devotes his entire attention to the theatre' (1927: 212). Quinn selects the playwright Gilbert Emery, a writer of 'new domestic dramas of character', as the 'model' against which Glaspell and Gale are found wanting (ibid.). More frequently it is the prolific output of O'Neill which is cited as evidence of Glaspell's theatrical shortcomings. This fails to acknowledge the sexual politics of theatre which disadvantages women, or even to perceive that women's lives are patterned quite differently to men's (a dominant thematic and stylistic concern of Glaspell's theatre). As Dymkowski has argued, 'to those who will retort that Glaspell gave up the theatre ... while O'Neill went on from strength to strength, the answer is simply that gender contributed to those developments as well' (1988: 102). Dymkowski's accompanying endnote to this statement also stresses that Glaspell's 'productive years coincided with her involvement in an amateur group which, besides supporting new writers, was equally open to women as to men' (105, n.23). This claim can be substantiated in a critical examination of the Provincetown Players in the early 1920s, the period in the history of the company when there was a shift from their amateur subscription stage in Macdougal Street to 'uptown' commercial venues.

The production of O'Neill's *The Emperor Jones* (1920) is cited by Deutsch and Hanau as the moment when New York 'found the Provincetown Players' with the help of the press whose 'support was instantaneous and almost unbelievable' (1931: 63). The authors quote from Heywood Broun's review in the *Tribune*, 4 November 1920, which lauded O'Neill as 'the most promising playwright in America' (65), and from Alexander Woollcott's review for the *New York Times*, 7 November 1920, which stated that O'Neill's play endorsed 'the impression that for strength and originality he has no rival among the American writers for the stage' (67). With the power of the press behind the production, O'Neill's *The Emperor Jones* was able to move 'uptown' and on to commercial stages. It was a controversial move to make given the company's commitment to the pioneering of 'new drama', and there were those, like Cook, who were fiercely opposed to the change (not least because the opening of the first full-length play he had written in years, *The Spring*, coincided with the commercial transfer of O'Neill's second play in the 1920–1 season, *Diff'rent*, thereby impoverishing the company left behind to perform his own drama in the 'downtown' venue: see Deutsch and Hanau 1931: 76).

Glaspell's political play *The Inheritors* performed in the same season as O'Neill's *The Emperor Jones* had a deservedly mixed reception. Although Glaspell tackled a radical subject (the play examines three generations of American libertarians in a way which raises controversial issues connected with the post-war government in America), she did so within a conventional form. Critical opinions ranged from J. Ranken Towse's favourable 'a dramatist of ideas has taken her place in the theatre' (*Evening Post*, March 1921, p. 9), to Woollcott's openly misogynous view of Glaspell's theatre:

> Miss Glaspell has thought it all out, and then poured her thought promiscuously into a watery play, more completely undramatic than any the season has seen – a play as artless as one a high school girl might dash off for commencement, as helplessly garrulous as poor old Miss Bates in 'Emma'.
>
> (*New York Times*, 27 March 1921, p. 1)

The male response to *The Inheritors* was, however, overall more favourable than the view of Glaspell's *The Verge* which opened the 1921–2 season, and which is arguably her most woman-centred drama. The pattern of an 'uptown' transfer had now been established, and was announced before the first performance of *The Verge* (see Deutsch and Hanau 1931: 85), but it played 'unprofitable matinees at the Garrick' and was brought back to the Provincetown 'downtown' venue to support an ailing season. There is no suggestion in Deutsch and Hanau's account of the different production histories of the Provincetown plays in this period that Glaspell could have raised funds independently to support a commercial venture for her work, as her husband did for his own play *The Spring*, which failed to attract audiences when he engineered its transfer to the Princess Theatre shortly before the opening of *The Verge* (ibid.: 84). The move from amateur to commercial stage was a possibility for the potential 'star' actress, as was evidenced in the case of Ann Harding who played the leading 'discontented heroine' role in Glaspell's *The Inheritors*, and was subsequently 'snatched up by other managers and launched on her spectacular career' (ibid.: 79). But for the female dramatist the transition was far more difficult, unless her 'star' vehicles could be 'read' as commercially viable.

O'Neill had managed to create star roles in both *The Emperor Jones* and *The Hairy Ape* which played in March 1922, and financially rescued the season which *The Verge* had opened. In the case of *The Emperor Jones* it was the professional (star) actor who made the role a success. The Black actor Charles Gilpin who took the part of Brutus Jones, and was chosen because of his colour, was the first professional performer to appear for the Players. In addition to Gilpin's star status, the role itself, although it appears to offer a radical edge, ultimately reaffirms rather than challenges dominant ideologies of race and ethnicity in its portrait of the 'emperor' who is oppressed but also oppresses. In *The Hairy Ape* O'Neill's leading role 'Yank' was also 'peculiarly suited' to Louis Wolheim who played it, and 'after this spectacular début and "What Price Glory?" in 1924, his rise in the theater was rapid' (Deutsch and Hanau 1931: 87). Moreover, if O'Neill's drama was seen to have its faults, as was the case with *The Hairy Ape*, these were forgiven by the critics for the promise he showed in becoming the new force the American stage so vitally needed. Contrast, for example, Woollcott's misogynous reviewing of Glaspell's *The Inheritors*, as previously cited, with his description of O'Neill's *The Hairy Ape* as a play 'so full of blemishes that the merest fledgling among the critics could point a dozen, yet so vital and interesting that those playgoers who let it escape them will be missing one of the real events of the year' (quoted in Deutsch and Hanau 1931: 87).

Because Glaspell's women did not conform to the dominant views on gender, they met with critical hostility and could not therefore make the same transition on to the mainstream stage as was the case with O'Neill's drama. Glaspell's gradual retreat from theatre following the death of her husband, and her return to fiction writing, can therefore be argued as an economic necessity: continuing a career in writing offered the possibility of relative financial independence, whereas a career in commercial dramatic writing for a woman did not (see Ozieblo 1990: 75).

THE VERGE

The marginalization of women's theatre due to the en-gendered approach of male reviewing can be specifically illustrated in an examination of contemporary (male) criticism of Glaspell's *The Verge* (1921).

The Verge has been described by feminist criticism as Glaspell's 'most provocative' and 'most impiously feminist play' (Ozieblo 1990: 70, 72). The play dramatizes the expression of a 'female' desire for life patterns different to those of men through its portrait of Claire Archer and her attempts to create new plant forms. Read at a metaphorical level Claire's botanical concerns reflect her quest for 'life': to escape from old conventions, patterns, etc., which are deadening and threaten to destroy life. She is surrounded by several male characters: her husband Harry, a former lover Richard Demming, and a current admirer Tom Edgeworthy. Tom (as his name suggests) comes the closest to understanding Claire's desire for 'otherness', but he cannot follow her far enough. The play closes with Claire choking Tom to death on stage, in order to save herself from being with a man who is *not enough*, and, through her murderous act, gives him the 'gift' of life (Glaspell 1987: 99).

The American critics could no more understand Claire than their European counterparts had been able to understand Ibsen's Nora Helmer or Hedda Gabler. Claire is repeatedly judged by them to be 'neurotic', 'insane', or 'abnormal'. The position of the critic is mirrored in the play itself by the views of the conventional characters (mostly male, but who also include Claire's sister and daughter) who are unable to comprehend Claire's desires. Her husband Harry in dialogue with Richard (Dick) Demming in the opening act, for example, elaborates on his inability to understand his wife and her botanical enterprises. Out in Claire's greenhouse, where the household and guests are assembled because Claire has directed all the heat out there to take care of her plants, the two men talk over what they perceive as Claire's peculiarities:

HARRY: Oh, I wish Claire wouldn't be strange like that. (*helplessly*) What is it? What's the matter?

DICK: It's merely the excess of a particularly rich temperament.

HARRY: But it's growing on her. I sometimes wonder if all this (*indicating the place around him*) is a good thing. It would

be all right if she'd just do what she did in the beginning –
make the flowers as good as possible of their kind. That's
an awfully nice thing for a woman to do – raise flowers.
But there's something about this – changing things into
other things – putting things together and making queer
new things – this –

DICK: Creating?

HARRY: Give it any name you want it to have – it's unsettling
for a woman. They say Claire's a shark at it, but what's the
good of it, if it gets her? ... I'd like to have Charlie
Emmons see her – he's fixed up a lot of people shot to
pieces in the war. Claire needs something to tone her
nerves *up*. You think it would irritate her?

(Glaspell 1987: 65)

The cultivation and arrangement of flowers is womanly. The
desire to create new plant forms is seen as 'queer', unwomanly,
and abnormal – and in need of being treated and cured by a male
nerve specialist. Claire as a woman in need of being cured was the
dominant view of the critics. Woollcott, reviewing for the *New
York Times*, declared her 'a study of an abnormal and neurotic
woman', and expressed his bewilderment over why the male
characters should show an interest in her at all:

It is not the authenticity of the portrait at which the average
passerby will strain and choke. It is the author's own
reverent, heroine-worshiping attitude towards this particular manifestation of the divine discontent ... which pro-
vokes combativeness in the onlooker. No one who has read
a little or listened a little in this fermenting city but will
recognize in part, at least, the woman now reared on the
Provincetown stage through the quickening touch of Mar-
garet Wycherly. What he will have more difficulty in recognizing is the three men who hotly pursue this distressed and
distressing lady instead of running from her as if she were
plague-stricken.

(*New York Times*, 15 November 1921)

The expression of hostility towards the portrait of Claire is,
however, an indication of the threat which she poses to the
position of male 'superiority' and 'authority' (see Ozieblo 1990:
66). Her desire to break out of 'prison' is of necessity a violent one.

Ibsen's slamming of the door in *A Doll's House* is replaced by the murder of the man who threatens to imprison Claire in another stultifying heterosexual relationship. Quinn's reaction to the violence of *The Verge* is typical:

> If there is one coherent idea in the play it is that only through violent suffering and wreckage of lives can any growth be attained. As this does not happen to be true the play fails by the test of verity.
>
> (1927: 211)

O'NEILL'S MEN AND GLASPELL'S WOMEN: FEMINIST READINGS

One of the few contemporary critics to acknowledge the engendering of Glaspell's work was Isaac Goldberg. He described her as 'the playwright of woman's selfhood' (1922: 474), and further compared and contrasted the work of O'Neill and Glaspell on a gender basis. In particular, with reference to the composition of character by the two dramatists, he stated that 'O'Neill's women do not understand their menfolk' and 'Glaspell's men do not understand their women' (477). It is an important distinction to make because it identifies, to use Goldberg's terms, O'Neill's concern with the 'masterful man' as opposed to Glaspell's interest in the 'rebellious woman' (472): the former supports the interests of patriarchy, the latter opposes it.

Modern feminist readings of O'Neill and Glaspell have explored this difference in representations of gender. Feminist approaches to O'Neill have examined how 'the female characters ... are defined ... by their relationships to the men in their lives' (Nelson 1982: 3). (Nelson's essay is one of six pieces which constitute a 'special section' entitled 'O'Neill's Women', in the *Eugene O'Neill Newsletter*.) Feminist critiques of narrative, à la De Lauretis, have challenged conventional readings of O'Neill's ability to portray 'feminine suffering', and instead have shown the ways in which O'Neill's male narratives refuse the female character a subject position. Anne Flèche, for example, has re-read the 'feminine "text" of Mary Tyrone' in *Long Day's Journey into Night* to demonstrate 'her objectification as a product of male narrative' (1989: 26). Subjectivity and narrative have also been central to feminist understandings of Glaspell's theatre and its representation of the 'female' position of 'otherness' (see Ben-Zvi 1986; Aston 1994). Where contemporary critics had taken issue with Glaspell for her lack of words, for being a dramatist a 'little afraid of speech' (Lewisohn 1932: 393), feminist analysis, in the wake of French feminist theory, has been able to understand Glaspell's use of language as a demonstration of her rejection of the 'symbolic' and desire for the 'semiotic'. Claire Archer's unfinished sentences, her inversion of meaning (for sanity read insanity, for normal read abnormal), and her desire to get underneath words are all evidence of this. Glaspell's women on the margins, locked in/out of language, represent the inability of the 'female' self to take a place.

Finally, feminist readings of Glaspell's theatre have also indicated that a re-evaluation of her theatre might also include an examination of her impact and influence on O'Neill. Contemporary production histories of the Provincetown Players do not consider, for example, that O'Neill's theatre owed much to Glaspell's scenic vision (see Ben-Zvi 1986; Larabee 1990). Ben-Zvi argues persuasively for the influence of Glaspell's *The Verge* on O'Neill's *The Hairy Ape*, and locates the sphere of influence specifically in the use of expressionistic settings. Ben-Zvi's comparative analysis also proposes an affinity between the two dramatists based on their shared 'pioneering thrust' as a 'central paradigm' in their theatre (1986: 24). Such an approach challenges what Radel (1990) exposes as the dominant Euro-centric approach to the O'Neill canon: the framing of O'Neill's work within European influences. Radel, however, argues that such an approach is 'gender-biased' because it fails to consider the home-based influence of American dramatists with whom O'Neill was working in his early, formative years, a number of whom were women (41).

This line of enquiry would also serve to re-evaluate Glaspell's contributions to staging which her contemporary critics universally overlooked. Modern critical preoccupation with the literary, with Glaspell as a dramatist, has meant that her work as an actress, as a director, has not been fully considered, and is still 'hidden'. To discover Glaspell as a performer, as a director, would make a valuable addition to the modern 'history' of feminist theatrical practice.

9

'BODILY HARM'

This case study takes three plays to examine some of the different theoretical positions and performance styles which feminist theatre may take to 'persuade' the spectator of its message. Through critical practice the study returns to a number of the feminist concerns that were raised in Part One of this study. The three plays selected share the focus of 'bodily harm': in their different ways they illustrate how the female body is a site/sight of male violence in systems of representation. The analysis of *Steaming* returns to the problematics of dramatizing a feminist dynamic in a classic realist form; *Heresies* provides an illustration of representing a community of women defined as 'Other' than men; and *Masterpieces* is examined as a theatrical text which combines a radical-feminist politics with a materialist practice. It must be stressed that the readings offered in the case studies, here as elsewhere, are not designed to be definitive. Rather, they complement the surveying of feminist concepts and methodologies in Part One; they provide examples of reading feminist theatre texts through different theoretical positions, without seeking to propose such readings as singular or absolute.

STEAMING

Nell Dunn's *Steaming*, first performed at The Theatre Royal, Stratford, London in 1981, takes place on the women-only days in 'the "Turkish" Rest Room of a 1909 Public Baths' (Dunn 1981: 9). The setting therefore creates a female 'space'. At a metaphorical level it represents the 'space' women need to recover from the everyday pressures of male oppression. Violet, the female attendant at the baths, takes care of her 'ladies': the hard-up, working-class Josie; the affluent but divorced Nancy; Nancy's friend Jane, a mature student trying to make it on her own; the elderly Mrs Meadows and her 'simple' daughter Dawn. All of the women enter the 'space' suffering from outside 'male' pressures which are symbolically represented in the only male character Bill: 'a man who is heard but not seen', whose 'absent presence' is suggested by his shadow which appears behind the glass door entry to the space. Each woman coming into the 'space' has her own life story to tell, and the individual narratives, woven together, structure the dominant discourse of patriarchal oppression.

In narrative terms the metaphorical 'space' of *Steaming* may also be read as the 'closed' (female) space (see De Lauretis on Lotman's narrative chain: Chapter 3 p. 40), which the 'male' hero penetrates, crosses, or passes through. While on the surface the play appears to refuse the 'male' access to the 'space', at another level the 'male' remains the initiator and subject of the narrative. The subject of each woman's story, for instance, is male: Josie narrates her violent relations with men; Nancy describes how her husband left her; Jane talks about trying to live without men; Mrs Meadow speaks of how she was infantilized by her husband; and Dawn, her daughter, is represented as part of a rape narrative. As storytellers the women appear in 'male drag'. They remain oppositionally defined in relation to men, and what they explore is their experience of being objects of exchange in the male economy: wives, mistresses, mothers, daughters, etc. Typical is this exchange between Josie and Nancy:

> NANCY: Yes . . . just for a while I felt a real woman . . . but most of my marriage I was just trying to make up the sort of person who did everything right . . . even in bed . . . it didn't occur to me I could ask for what I wanted . . .
> JOSIE: So you never told him how you really felt? . . .
> NANCY: I did try telling him once and he said, 'Don't upset me now, I've got a very heavy work load on'.
> JOSIE: You shouldn't have let him get away with that . . . You should have yelled at him . . . 'What are you then, a man or a toad! . . . You're supposed to be my husband and I'm your wife!' That's what I used to say to my old man . . .
>
> (Dunn 1981: 44)

During the course of the play the baths come under threat of

121

closure by the local authorities and the women are unsuccessful in their attempts to have the decision to close the baths overturned. As a form of protest they lock themselves into the 'space'. This fight to save the baths is emblematic of the bourgeois-feminist approach which proposes that the amelioration of women's position in society may be achieved through legislative change. That the women are defeated in their opposition to the council's legislation for closure demonstrates the difficulties, and ultimately the ineffectiveness of this course of (political) action, which does nothing to alter the unequal male/female power relations. Given this outcome, Jane's impassioned plea for the bourgeois-feminist case has a rather hollow ring to it: 'You see, we've got to believe we really are as important as they [men] are, not better, not worse, but just as important!' (44).

Thematically, too, the play centrally explores areas of women's lives in which they are confined and controlled by men: body image, sexuality, marriage, domesticity, education, etc. Dunn's feminist critique of these male systems of control offers fleeting moments of optimism: as Josie gains the confidence to speak at the protest; as Dawn discovers the freedom to enjoy her body without her 'plastics'; as the women dine together in the baths and indulge in the forbidden pleasures of eating, etc. None of these, however, will effect any radical transformation of the women's lives. Most telling in this respect is the play's failure to engage with a gender and class critique.

Class issues are touched on – particularly in relation to the working-class portrait of Josie, but the intra-sexual dynamic militates against developing a gender and class-based analysis. For example, in the 'class' confrontation staged between Nancy and Josie in Act Two: Scene One, the different material circumstances of the two women are cited as an area of difference. Ultimately, however, it is suggested that both women are the 'same', as both women are dependent upon men for access to economic power and financial security:

NANCY: (*turns to face Josie and says slowly and deliberately*)
Perhaps I didn't leave him because I had a lovely home, a lovely garden. I saw no way I could keep myself and my children in the manner to which we were accustomed . . . I had no money!
JOSIE: Oh . . . you sound a bit like me!

NANCY: I've never realized that before ... (*She bursts out laughing.*)

(Dunn 1981: 58)

The radical edge to a class critique is, therefore, undermined. The possibility of exploring intra-sexual oppression is excluded, as is a critique of class-based power relations. It is even suggested at one point that women are to blame for their oppression: that it is 'our [women's] fault' (63).

As the women's stories are imprisoned within the mainstream narrative structures of realism, the female performer is invited to adopt the actor–character identification method of acting. That this detracts from any possible manifestation of a feminist performance style is demonstrated by the way in which the dramatic and theatrical texts position the spectator as author of the 'male gaze'. The spectator is required to gaze on the female bodies – quite literally in this instance, as the stage directions indicate the bodies are often to be naked – in a way which reinforces the dominant (male) ideology of the 'body beautiful'. Keyssar has commented as follows:

> The play risks disturbing audience biases by requiring us to acknowledge the naked bodies of women over thirty-five. Unfortunately, in the West End production, rather than establishing the common vulnerability of women, nudity was used to titillate the audience. The act of disrobing was played to the audience with an inappropriate coyness; lighting, blocking and costuming called attention to breasts; and pacing called attention to the rarity of undressing on stage. *Steaming* yields, unnecessarily, to one of the dangers of feminist theatre, that it makes the audience voyeurs of secret women's worlds rather than participant–observers in a complex social-sexual structure.
>
> (1984: 156)

It may be argued that the commercial success of plays like *Steaming* which fall into the dominant stage traditions of realism and realistic acting styles help to create more roles for women in mainstream theatrical contexts, and that such an achievement works towards redressing the imbalance in the work ratios in theatre which favour men and disadvantage women. That said, it is also the case that performing the mainstream may be argued as a retrogressive, even oppressive, mode of practice in relation to the possibility of women taking up a subject position in the theatrical frame and subverting the gaze.

HERESIES

Deborah Levy's *Heresies* was the first production by the British RSC's women's group in 1986. Given the cultural status of the RSC and the style of their work, Levy's theatre represents a significant challenge to and departure from the more conventional 'strong-roles-for-women' approach one might expect from a female splinter group of the mainstream theatrical 'establishment'.

Heresies is woven out of a number of quest-based narratives. The dominant quest-based actantial model in which the subject (male) quests the object (female) is encoded in the quest of the architect Pimm to recover his daughter, Lydia, and her mother, Cholla, who had left him shortly after the baby was born. Pimm's male quest, however, collides with other quest-based narratives en-acted through female agents seeking to determine their own lives, and the lives of other women, in a way which frees them from their 'object' positioning in the male quest. Cholla, the Displaced Person, is central to this quest, and is helped by a pairing of older women: Leah, the Composer, and Violet, the Educator. The interweaving of the male and female narratives creates a site of gender struggle. In contrast to *Steaming*, however, it is the sphere of the 'feminine' which subverts the gaze: the (Symbolic) Law of the Father.

The narratives unfold in a dramatic fictional present which Levy describes as a mixing of two time planes: 'the future and the past'. As Levy explains:

The future is the world the architect is constructing – i.e. post-modern, materials being steel and glass, for example.

The past is the world the composer and educator inhabit – i.e. a battered old grand piano, lace, wind chimes.

There are no scene changes. All characters will pass through these two worlds – the past and the future.

(Levy 1987: Production Notes)

The time past which Leah and Violet inhabit may be read in Kristevan terms as the cyclical and the monumental. They give expression to women's experiences 'left mute by culture in the past' (see p. 54), and so resist and refuse the linearity of the male quest: the future built on the silence, destruction, and death of the female subject.

The set notes also give an indication of Levy's style which is resistant to the 'prisonhouse of realism'. Levy's own physical theatre training at Dartington College of Arts has fostered her concern to explore all the languages of the stage, and especially the physical language of the performer. This means creating a performance language which consists of much more than the spoken word of the playscript: 'Theatre is not English literature. It is a kinetic fusion of, one hopes, eloquent language – some of which is spoken. Text, image and action must be as articulate as each other' (Levy 1992: 2). Moreover, the language of *Heresies* is a fusion of image, music, and text which fragments and resists the symbolic. Kristeva has described how:

> the silent theater of colors, sounds and gestures, sends the subject back to that region of the structure of the speaking being where a lethal drive operates, a drive of forgetfulness or of death, which I have called the *semiotic*.
>
> (1977: 132)

Levy has scenes of music and sounds which explore the region of the semiotic, or Lacanian Imaginary, before the entry into the symbolic. Scenes Eight, Ten, and Twelve in Act One, for example, centre on music and sounds orchestrated by Leah and Violet. Scene Eight is set out as follows:

> *Leah plays something 'birdlike' on her piano. The musicians pick up on her theme. Lights on Violet, whose memory has been stirred.*
> VIOLET (very softly but unmistakably birdlike): KwaaaKrrrrr-KwarrrrKwarrr Kwarrr . . .
> *Piano, violin, and flute.*
>
> (Levy 1987: 10)

However, scenes connected with Pimm's quest for his daughter and her mother cut across these moments: the Symbolic Order of paternal law represses the semiotic, though cannot keep it from pulsating and breaking through.

Heresies has two main male agents of paternal law: Pimm the architect and Edward 'the lonely business man'. Their desire for self-definition, self-fulfilment, is an expression of Cixous's Hegelian analysis of the 'Selfsame (*Propre*)' (Cixous and Clément 1987 [1975]: 79). In such a scheme:

125

there is no place for the other, for an equal other, for a whole and living woman. She must recognize and recuntnize the male partner, and in the time it takes to do this, she must disappear, leaving him to gain Imaginary profit, to win Imaginary victory. (ibid.)

As the 'Selfsame' is built on fear, the fear of the 'not-selfsame, not-mine', then the subject in this scheme experiences the desire to 'reappropriate', to make its 'mastery felt' (Cixous and Clément: 80). Edward seeks to appropriate his wife, Mayonnaise. He desires 'a monopoly on her love' in order for him to feel real and alive (Levy 1987: 13). Pimm desires to reappropriate Cholla/Lydia which is expressive of the desire to master Cholla's historical and cultural identity as an Eastern (she is Hungarian) woman. The colonizing, imperialist impulse is a condition of the Western Law of the Father/phallus. Pimm 'colonizes' his Irish servant Mary, and seeks to enslave Cholla, in order to reaffirm his sense of self, his position of masculine power.

Cholla, as a displaced person, is homeless. Having left Pimm she has freed herself from her position as 'other' in the male economy of desire, but is seeking to be re-located, re-made in an economy of the 'feminine'. This the play effects in its closure by bringing together all of the female characters in the final scene, and articulating the possibility of Cholla's return to the East. By contrast, Mayonnaise who is not only married to Edward but is also Pimm's mistress, seeks to trade herself as 'currency' in the economic transactions between men (see Irigaray 1981 [1977]: 107). Levy assigns her the label 'courtesan'. As the property of her husband she functions as hostess and is materially provided for. As the property of Pimm she constructs herself as valuable object. The violence en-acted against her in this exchange, however, is designated in her name (she explains to Cholla that she is called Mayonnaise because she has 'often been beaten for a very long time'; Levy 1987: 29), and represented in the disintegration of her body, which is made manifest in her eating disorders (the result of trying to keep her body beautiful and 'flawless'), and the gradual loss of her hair.

While part of this economy Mayonnaise is represented as alone. She does not bond with the other women. Rather, she functions as a male agent, and adopts the values of the masculine, as further illustrated in her 'mastering' and oppression of Pimm's servant

Mary. Betty, her mother, who comes looking for the daughter she abandoned years ago, is similarly constructed. Both women, however, ultimately side against the masculine by helping Cholla. In the final scene Mayonnaise is the last to join the community of women, but when she appears she is completely bald: a visual sign of the 'bodily harm' inflicted on women constructed as Woman in the economy of the (male) gaze. 'The courtesan has been stripped' states Mayonnaise as the other women come forward to *touch her head as if to heal her*' (30).

Cixous asks: 'In the Selfsame Empire, where will the displacement's person find somewhere to lose herself, to write her not-taking-place, her permanent availability' (Cixous and Clément 1987: 97). Levy's play allows the 'other', that which is marginalized, oppressed, and made invisible in the symbolic, to be made visible in the space of the past inhabited by Leah and Violet. Gradually, as the women refuse the symbolic they are drawn towards the semiotic. Mary who 'mothers' her sister Bridie (imprisoned for her protest against the British soldiers in Ireland) leaves Pimm's service. Cholla refuses to re-enter the symbolic and entrusts the care of her child to Leah and Violet. On the other hand, Pimm visits Leah, his former teacher, but cannot relate to her, and Edward is left alone in a tableau of suicide and despair.

It is Leah, coupled with Violet, who represents the pre-Oedipal mother of the Imaginary. Leah's music is her homeland, her roots. She has found her music in the sea. In the final scene Levy's instructions for Leah's music which close the play are as follows:

> *Sound of whales, sea, wind. The composition is an eclectic collage of classical disciplines, avant-garde explorations, the resonance of non-western instruments. It is more atonal than melodic. It is restless, witty, celebratory. It is haunting and uncompromising. It can last up to five minutes.*
>
> (Levy 1987: 30)

The return to 'the mother/the sea' is, as Cixous describes and Levy enacts, 'the song of women being brought into the world' (Cixous 1984: 547).

Leah and Violet hold the keys to women's culture, to women's past, which has been silenced by men. As the women gather for Leah's concert it is her wish that the work she has begun be finished by them: the return to 'the mother/the sea' is an invitation to a very different future.

MASTERPIECES

In a recent interview Levy characterized her sense of a 'female language' in theatre as 'attention, not intention. It's where your attention is as a writer' (Levy 1993: 228). Sarah Daniels is a playwright whose 'attention' to women takes a different route, one which has earned her the hostility of many male (and some female) critics. Writing in the introduction to Methuen's sixth volume of *Plays by Women*, Mary Remnant, taking issue with the way in which Sarah Daniels has been 'characterised by many [male] critics as the venom-spitting virago of radical feminist theatre', describes her as 'one of the very few – some would say the most notorious – of women playwrights in Britain to have reached mainstream audiences' (1987: 7). *Masterpieces* (first performed in 1983 at the Royal Exchange Theatre, Manchester, and the Royal Court Theatre Upstairs, London) is a hard-hitting and powerful feminist attack on pornography which outraged and 'wounded' a number of 'masculine sensitivities' among the critics:

> Critics reviewing *Masterpieces* declared that there was no proven connection between pornography and violence against women, and implied that it was only a few nasty perverts who were being so beastly anyway. Amidst a growing awareness of the part played by anti-black, anti-Irish and anti-Semitic jokes in perpetuating racism, the critics dug in their heels and insisted that the very idea that misogynist jokes had anything to do with misogyny was patently ridiculous. Daniels' anger was merely a 'cascade of bile' (Shulman) and her 'scream of outrage' (Wardle) was drowned out by their own.
>
> (Remnant 1987: 8)

Masterpieces represents an important contribution to the feminist debate on pornography. There are two positions which have been taken up by feminists over this issue: the anti-pornography campaign, and, more recently, as Dolan explains, a position 'represented by feminists who are prosex and who support the cultural production of sexual fantasies' (Dolan 1988: 59. For a discussion of these two positions see Kappeler 1986). In *Masterpieces* Daniels adopts the anti-pornography position. Her radical-feminist critique covers a range of pornographic practices – from misogynist jokes to snuff movies. In the introduction to her seminal study on pornography, anti-pornography campaigner Andrea Dworkin states that 'the ways and means of pornography are the ways and means of male power' (1981: 24). *Masterpieces* is a radical-feminist exploration of pornography as a source of 'male power' and an examination of the possible effects it has on the lives of women. Whilst the play's political line is radical-feminist in its attack on patriarchy, the methods of theatricalization owe much to the Brechtian model, and the radical critique combines with materialist practice.

Rowena, the central protagonist in *Masterpieces*, is used to illustrate the devastating effects which systems of representation (women represented as Woman) have on women's lives. Abused and violated by such systems, Rowena pushes away a man who is harassing her at a London tube station. He falls on to the track, is killed, and Rowena is charged with 'murder'. As Case states: 'the object status of women in the system incites a woman to violence against her victimizer' (1991: 241). Case continues:

the murder near the end of the play illustrates the violence of the battle women must wage to take back their own bodies from the scopophilic male gaze and the discourse that turns them into a target for sexualized aggression.

(ibid.)

Wandor's criticism of *Masterpieces* appears to miss this point. She criticizes the play for the little space women have together in it, for the way in which it apparently accepts 'that power is held by men and is unchallengeable', and for what she characterizes as its 'soft-edged radical feminism' (Wandor 1984b: 90–1). This fails to acknowledge that the central narrative of *Masterpieces* is the narrative of 'looking-at-being-looked-at-ness'. The play is not a 'soft-edged' critique of the gaze, but an intervention in its production. The use of critical distancing techniques (see below) empower the spectator to refuse the objectification of women and to 'see' them differently.

Masterpieces, therefore, not only takes issue with pornography in the form of dirty magazines, nasty videos, snuff movies, etc. but alienates the ways in which women are objectified in systems of social and cultural representation and de-automatizes the spectator's response to the 'naturalization' of gender oppression. As Rowena's friend Yvonne tries to explain to her: 'Men, it's all to do with the way men are taught to view women' (Daniels 1984: 40).

Whilst the play ends with Rowena's account of the violence against women in a snuff movie, it begins with a dinner party scene in which the men crack misogynist jokes which the women are required to laugh at. Jennifer, Rowena's mother, laughs excessively at the men's jokes, much to the discomfort and embarrassment of the other dinner guests, but it is a laughter which de-familiarizes the common position of women who are forced into the position of laughing in spite of themselves. It is a laughter which speaks the 'but I am not that'.

Daniels makes use of the classic realist style in her construction of scenes only to have it shot through and disrupted by an interrogative mode which resists the 'prisonhouse of realism', thereby avoiding the problems which *Steaming* falls into. The linear narrative model which progresses and works towards closure is reversed: Rowena is already on trial in the opening scene. The conventions of the court room drama which create tension around the outcome are undermined. It is not what happened but why it happened which is the concern. In addition to stylistic shifts, distancing techniques also include shifts in narrative time and location, the use of monologues, and direct address.

In terms of alienating the female body in systems of representation, Daniels uses techniques which fragment or take the body out of the frame. In Scene Eight Rowena asks to look at the pornographic magazines which Yvonne has confiscated from the boys in her school. The stage directions indicate that Rowena is to look at the magazines in such a way that the audience does not see their images, etc. As she looks at the magazines a tape of three female monologues is played, but the voices heard on the tape are not, Daniels instructs, the voices of women in the cast (41). Each monologue is the narrative of a woman involved in pornography and each narrative speaks of the degradation involved when women trade their bodies as a 'commodity' (42). The monologues allow the narrative of objectification from the female point of view, which is repressed in the dominant trajectory of male desire, to be made 'visible'. The alienation of voice and body prevents the re-assimilation of the female into the male economy of desire.

Earlier in the play, in Scene Five, Daniels shows Rowena out late at night after visiting her client Hilary:

10 p.m. Rowena is walking home after her last visit. A man walks behind her. (This is quite 'innocent'. There is no threat of attack.) Rowena and the man freeze, then walk again.

130

ROWENA (*voice over*): Wish I wasn't wearing skirt. I look quite respectable though. What am I doing out this late at night? Working. The only women who work at night are prostitutes. Otherwise their husbands would meet them. Don't walk fast, it will look funny. Don't slow up – inviting. Don't look too nervous. Why the hell doesn't he cross over. *They pass each other. They look back.*

(25–6)

The freeze-framing and voice-over techniques critically foreground the possibility of male attack and Rowena's complicity in assessing her self-presentation on male terms.

The threat of rape is realized later in the play when Rowena secures Hilary a job with Yvonne's husband, Ron. Ron harasses Hilary in the workplace and, the audience is given to understand, rapes her after giving her a lift home. The flashback, Scene Fifteen, in which Rowena hears an account of this from Hilary, is presented in the form of pre-recorded dialogue. Distance is therefore created through the use of the time shift and the vocal recording so that the spectator is not seduced into the narrative of victimization, but is required to critically reflect on it. Moreover, this scene is juxtaposed with Fourteen which re-enacts the scene at the tube station: time, space, and narrative dislocations alienate the violence against women which in male systems of representation is 'naturalized'.

Hilary is an important figure in *Masterpieces* in terms of extending the play's radical critique to a class analysis. Although this is not pursued as extensively as it might be, Daniels uses Hilary as a vehicle for demonstrating how, as a working-class single mother, Hilary is oppressed by her class background as well as her gender. Half-way through the play, Hilary's working-class voice is given the space of a scene-length monologue which cuts across the middle-class marriage scenes of the other women. Rowena's position as Hilary's social worker is highlighted as an example of intra-sexual oppression.

The class critique is not considered within the masculine discourse: all the male characters are middle-class misogynists. Capitalist as well as patriarchal concerns are, however, raised in the prologue to *Masterpieces*. This consists of three male monologues (the pornography baron, the pedlar, and the consumer) constructed in a way which invites the spectator to consider the material conditions in which pornography exists as a money-making 'industry' for capitalism.

The colonization of women's bodies which takes place in the traffic between the male producers and consumers of pornography, services the economy and the economy of male desire. The desire to 'master' which characterizes the 'bodily harm' dramatized in each of these three plays is explored further in the following case study which examines the processes of colonization in the context of race and gender oppression.

10

COLONIAL LANDSCAPES

I IS A LONG MEMORIED WOMAN: OVERVIEW AND STRUCTURE

This case study of the videotext based on the collection of poems *i is a long memoried woman* by Grace Nichols (1990a [1983]), is designed to complement the commentary on the methods and concepts of Black women's theatre in Britain discussed in Chapter 6. As a videotext, *i is a long memoried woman* (1990b) creates the opportunity for exploring a feminist critical practice in the context of production analysis, but most importantly demonstrates the materialist style and discourse of a performance text which makes visible the historical and material conditions of a racial and gender-based oppression.

The videotext draws on the poems, an interview with Grace Nichols, and archive material to present the her/history of the African-Caribbean slave woman, performed through the African theatrical form of storytelling, dance, and music (see Sears 1990: 96). This challenges the 'grand narratives' of 'European thought' (see p. 91), and Western traditions of theatrical form. In the interview material used in the videotext Nichols explains the purpose of her poetry collection as follows:

> The whole book is a journey of the Black woman uprooted from Africa and taken in captivity . . . The long memoried woman embodies all the experiences, the emotions, the feelings that any slave woman would have gone through, you know. She experiences all of that, but the important thing is that at the end of it she survives, you know. She survives, and in one sense the book is a celebration of the endurance, the vitality and the spiritual strength of the Black

woman of the diaspora. It was an horrific experience if you think about it, to be just uprooted like that from your society.
(Nichols 1990b)

The collection of poems tells the story of the long memoried slave woman in five parts: 'The Beginning', 'The Vicissitudes', 'The Sorcery', 'The Bloodling', and 'The Return'. The videotext selects poems from each of these parts, and creates a further section or sequence before 'The Return' entitled 'The Rebellion'.

In brief, 'The Beginning' narrates the 'Black Beginning', as it is described in the poem 'One Continent/To Another', of being born into slavery (Nichols 1990a: 5–7). It highlights the back-breaking work of the slave woman out in the fields of sugar cane. 'The Vicissitudes' speaks again of the pain of her life, and of the dreams she needs to hang on to as a way of surviving. As Nichols explains in the video interview:

> Her memory keeps shifting, you know, from joyful things and consoling things to the times when she's just going to feel despair because she's cut off, you know, from her/that environment – her homeland.
>
> (1990b)

'The Sorcery' illustrates how the slave woman's survival depends on the strength she draws from Africa and her traditions, and particularly from the traditions of sorcery and magic. This helps her to resist the oppression she suffers in the world around her: oppression at the hands of white masters and their wives, and the Black overseers.

The extent of her oppression is felt in 'The Bloodling' which tells of her birthing a child by the slave master. For comfort, for blessings, she calls upon the mother/the motherland to help her. Resistance is the theme of 'The Rebellion' part which follows. Nichols explains that the slave woman recognizes that no one will give her her freedom. She will have to take it. Here, the slave woman calls on the warrior figures of her culture/s: Ogun, the Ashanti priestess Nanny, etc. Finally, 'The Return' speaks of how the legacy of slavery means that Black women today remain connected to Africa. They live with what Nichols describes as a sense of journeying, of a restlessness born of the history mapped out between continents.

i is a long memoried woman therefore gives a voice to the slave woman whose history has been silenced by oppression. The pain of speaking is signalled in the title as the voice of the slave woman speaks her absence/presence, which, speaking, enters yet at the same time resists the symbolic. She is not 'I am', the singular, unified subject, but 'i is', the voice of the collective and frag-mented, who does not agree or conform, but rebels. The speaking voice is the voice of the woman who carries the painful memory of her past in the present. Moreover, Nichols explains how as a writer she works in both standard English and Creole – the language of the slaves which they developed as a means of communicating when they were taken away from their own African tribal languages. The language of slavery is set against the language of 'mastery' which it critiques.

By taking the collection of poetry as the basis of the videotext, the piece has a working structure which refuses the narrative, structural and ideological conventions and concerns of classic realism, which is alien to Black experience and Black culture. The 'parts' which make up the performance text do not progress in action and time towards closure. Rather, the narrative shifts in and out of the slave woman's memories: time is the past in the present. The memories write the experiences of female slavery into Western history which has silenced them, but the time in which they unfold is the monumental time of the slave woman's memory.

THE BLACK DIASPORA

The poetry of *i is a long memoried woman* is rooted in the oral traditions of African storytelling, and is spoken, chanted, and sung. It is voiced-over, works with and against images, and is fused with the music, choreographed movement, and dance of the piece. The delivery of the poetry is shared between two narrators: Adjoa Andoh and Leonie Forbes. They are joined by a third speaking voice: the voice of the poet. Nichols reads from some of her poetry and offers explanatory and contextualizing details of some of the individual poems. The insertion of the speaking voice of Nichols as writer is an important part of the 'text', because it writes into the performance the autobiographical dimension of Nichols as Black female poet living and working in Britain, but who also shares the memory of the slave woman. As Nichols explains in the video, in her British life she carries with her a past from Guyana: her 'text' is a form of Black oral history. This point is made in 'The Beginning' sequence as the camera uses an establishing shot to locate the spectator on the streets of London and then gradually, in close-up shots, focuses on young Black women out in the city. The focus, combined with the technique of slow-motion filming, singles them out, alienates them from the London crowd. Grace Nichols is filmed walking among them, and at the same time is heard speaking her poetry which overlays the visual text of 'being-Black-and-female-in-Britain-to-day' with an aural text which encodes the past, from another continent, in the present:

> From the darkness within her
> from the dimness of previous incarnations
>   the Congo surfaced
> so did Sierra Leone and the
> Gold Coast which she used to tread
> searching the horizons for lost
> moons
>
> (Nichols 1990a: 6)

As Zhana comments in the introduction to *Sojourn*, a collection of poetry and prose by Black women living in Britain today:

> It is impossible to talk about the Black presence in the British Isles in isolation. Discussion of our presence here immediately brings up issues of the slave trade and colonization. When writing about the community of Black British women, it is essential to do so in the context of other countries, the wider community of the Black diaspora.
>
> (1988: 11–12)

The landscape of 'the Black diaspora' is central to aesthetic and ideological concerns of *i is a long memoried woman*. The colonization of the slave woman between continents and cultures constitutes her multi-landscaped memory.

COLONIZING THE BODY

Colonial landscaping in the performance text is realized through a variety of techniques. The African landscape is imaged in the figures of tribal figures and gods; is evoked in the poetry, dance, music, song, and the rhythms of the African drums which haunt the diaspora. The sugar islands of the Caribbean are imaged in photography of the canefields, in dance tableaux, and suggested aurally in the percussion sounds of cutting cane. Black and white archival images of African and Caribbean landscapes reinforce the canvas of Black slavery and the 'mastery' of the white oppressor. The geography of colonization is most importantly and centrally landscaped or mapped on to the bodies of the performers. For example, in 'The Beginning' sequence the African woman, cleansing herself on her native shores, is taken in slavery to the Caribbean. This is imaged as follows: the African woman is caught in a sheet of cloth, is restrained and trapped like an animal netted by hunters. The image fades and cuts to black and white archival images of transportation scenes, then returns to an image of a Black woman's body which functions as a scenic sign to demonstrate the environment of the transportation ship. This is linked to a birthing image, as the woman/ship grips, and pulls the cloth out of which the 'child of the middle passage', the woman shipped between continents, emerges. The slave woman is born. Similarly, in the dance sequence which accompanies the poem 'Sugar Cane', the oppressive landscape of the canefields is established through the choreographed movements of the dancers.

The colonization of the body is also encoded in the vestimentary colour sign-system of the costuming. The Black dancers in the Caribbean landscape are costumed in white: Western oppression is signed on their bodies and encoded in their dance. The white tradition of classical dance is critiqued by the presence of the Black performer/body, and acts of racial oppression are ritually played out in dance sequences. To give a specific example: in the sequence 'Sorcery' the white oppression of the master's household is encoded in the appearance, costuming, and gestures of the performers. As Forbes narrates the poem 'Love Act' (see Nichols 1990a: 48–9), the second narrator, Andoh, signals her entry into the master's house by putting on a black apron of servitude. The master and mistress are role-played by two of the dancers: the male dancer is costumed as the master in top hat, white wig, and painted white face; the female dancer has similar make-up, and carries a parasol. The white painted faces alienate the Western performance tradition of 'blacking-up' in minstrel style, the colonizing of Black people as a form of entertainment for white audiences. The gestures and movements of the master and mistress signify mastery and dominance. The third Black dancer takes over the role of Black female servant from the narrator. Her rape by the master of the house is imaged in the slow-motion filming of the master pulling her to the ground by her hair. The technique of slow motion alienates the act of violence, as does the imaging of rape in the taking of the body by the hair. The mistress-figure is both aloof and looks on. She condones the violence because it temporarily frees her from the oppressive 'love act' with her husband, and the pregnancies which follow it.

The master/mistress role-playing is returned to later in the 'Sorcery' section, but in song and dance sequences which rebel against colonization. First, the narrators and musicians burst into a song about the 'buckra woman', the white mistress, and her 'buckra man' (see 'Hi De Buckras Hi!', Nichols 1990a: 43–4). The song, which mocks the white mistress in the finery of her dress, with her white skin shaded by her parasol, is accompanied by the parodic miming of the white woman's appearance and gestures. The white woman is metonymically represented by her parasol, which Andoh mockingly uses to image her with. Nichols explains the singing as one of the few permitted forms of expression available to the slave woman: a form of release going back to the African traditions of satirical song. The release of the slave woman is signalled in the music sequence by a change in mood and song. The rebel laughter of the slave woman is heard through the narrated lines of the poem 'Skin Teeth':

> Know that I smile
> know that I bend
> only the better
> to rise and strike
> again
> (Nichols 1990a: 50)

This is followed by the poem 'I Coming Back' which continues the theme of resistance and rebellion. The poem is chanted and accompanied by African drum rhythms; these are used to choreograph a dance sequence which returns to the triangle of master, mistress, and slave woman performed earlier. The parasol (mistress) is now in the hands of the dancer who plays the slave woman. The master takes it from her and returns it to his wife, and the slave woman is pushed down again. The master and mistress are seated on her back, but the slave woman rises up. She confronts the mistress and seizes the parasol. The dance becomes frenzied as the costuming of the master race, the props of the oppressor, are peeled off, and discarded.

BLACK CULTURE/BLACK HISTORY

An important part of resisting oppression is the recourse which the slave woman has to her culture and her history, which are written out of Western culture and Western history books. Keeping hold of African cultural traditions – the songs, the goddesses, the spiritual powers, etc. – empower the slave woman by offering her a source of comfort and resistance. 'The Rebellion' sequence theatricalizes mythical and historical figures which are the keys to a repressed Black culture and history. The Ashanti warrior queen, Nanny, believed to have the power to work magic against the white oppressor, is called upon by the long memoried woman to help her spill 'the red oppressors' blood' ('Nanny', Nichols 1990a: 73). Toussaint l'Ouverture, the Black slave who defeated Napoleon's army, is discussed by Nichols in the videotext as a symbol of Black pride and resistance (see '. . . And Toussaint', Nichols 1990a: 83–4). Nichols contrasts, however, the way in which William Wilberforce is well-known for his work on changing the laws of slavery, but Toussaint, a revolutionary symbol in Black history, has been made invisible. Black history and culture are important parts of the slave woman's memory, which the colonizing forces of Western history and culture desire to make her forget.

The Brewster interview (1991), cited in Chapter 6, contains an example which complements the point which Nichols makes. Brewster relates the anecdote of her being selected as the British representative for a New York Festival of Art which was to bring together different women directors from around the world to work on a project centred on Joan of Arc. A white, female British director might easily have found links or ways of identifying with this female warrior-figure celebrated in British history, but as a Black West Indian British woman, Brewster found it impossible to work on St. Joan, but could relate to the figure of the 'Woman Warrior' by drawing on the figure of Nanny. The famous Black American actresses who worked with her on this project, many of whom who had West Indian origins, had lost touch with their cultural ancestry. Working with Brewster on the figure of Nanny gave them a way back to a culture they had lost in American society whose values they had 'internalized' (see Brewster 1991: 365–6).

THE SLAVE-MOTHER

i is a long memoried woman also demonstrates that the Western concept of mother is alien to the experience of the slave woman. The Western celebration of mother and child as one, celebrated in the iconography of the baby at the breast, does not represent how the slave woman experienced being a mother. As Zhana writes:

> Slave women were often not even permitted to think of themselves as mothers. In Africa, Black women's primary role had been to be fertile, to produce children. They were proud of this role, which gave them status in society. As slaves in the Caribbean and the US, this role was perverted by white slavemasters who used Black women as breeders. They tried to break up the family unit by selling Black women's children away from them, and used this humiliation as a form of behaviour control to keep Black women in line. Black mothers saw their mother role debased.
>
> (1988: 65)

The long memoried woman recalls the painful experiences of motherhood: the slave-mother who kills her baby to set the child free from captivity; the birthing of a baby fathered by the white slave master. For the slave woman motherhood is characterized not by bonding, but by bondage; by the pain not of unity but of separation, as emblematized in her own enforced estrangement from Africa, the Motherland. For example, the birthing of the 'mulatto' in 'The Bloodling' sequence shows the slave woman in despair at the prospect of carrying the child of the white slave master. The slow-motion, superimposed, fragmented images of the slave woman (Andoh) visually encode and en-act the desperation which is tearing her body apart. Yet it is the spirit of the mother/motherland which helps her to survive. In the birthing sequence, Andoh is physically supported by Forbes whose gestures encode the giving of strength and the sharing of pain: she represents Africa, the 'mother' the slave woman has lost, but the 'mother' who is with her in her memory giving her comfort and strength. The sharing of the narration between Forbes, as an older woman, and Andoh, as a younger performer, is one which also underlines the suggestion of a mother/daughter relationship. Furthermore, the sense of Africa, the Motherland, is, as the Brewster anecdote demonstrates, an important part of the Black woman's social, cultural, and historical identity today. In 'The Return' sequence the voice of the African 'mother' (Forbes) 'enters', speaks to her daughter imaged in the city 'landscape' of London.

i is a long memoried woman plays in the 'gaps' of white history and culture to demonstrate the history and identity of the slave woman. The 'i' is the revolutionary 'i' of Black women: the 'i' who speaks but also resists oppression. The colonizing structure of the classic realist form is refused. The narrative voice which is singular and authoritative is destabilized by the narration of the two Black women. Language, 'master' of the symbolic, gives way to a language and aesthetic which fuses poetry, music, and dance. The 'presence' of the slave woman is not fetishized or 'fixed': traces of her remembered history enter and leave the frame in different bodies, different voices, but she refuses to be re-enslaved in the systems of representation. In her smile the repressed traces of her rebel gaze are made visible:

> From dih pout
> of mih mouth
> from dih
> treacherous
> calm of mih
> smile
> you can tell
> i is a long memoried woman.
> (Nichols 1990a: 3)

141

11

PERFORMING ROMANTIC CRITICISM
Case study and conclusion

PERFORMING FEMINIST CRITICISM

In her description of the 'new field theory' of feminist theatre studies, the subject of this study, Case states that it is a field which 'enables the critic to perceive recent plays by women playwrights, recent feminist theory, and recent discoveries in critical methodology as interactive and interdependent within the last two decades of the liberation of the feminine gender' (1989a: 126). It is important to recognize, therefore, that as an interactive model of plays, theory, and criticism, the field of feminist theatre studies may be able to offer other fields of study valuable 'ways of feminist seeing'.

Currently, however, there exists a 'gap' between women's studies and theatre studies. Gayle Austin has recently stated that drama and performance:

> has barely been tapped as a source of material by the field of women's studies. Women comfortable with the idea of interdisciplinary work still shy away from using dramatic texts, preferring to draw theories from and analyze prose, poetry, or film texts.
>
> (1990: 2)

It is possible that the 'gap' between the two fields has arisen because of the academic history of feminism and theatre studies as outlined in Chapter 1. The late development of theatre studies as a discipline, the fight for autonomy from English studies, which Reinelt and Roach describe as 'politically necessary' (1992: 5), has meant that the feminist agenda in theatre studies has been isolated from feminist spheres of activity in other disciplines, and, consequently, has not been taken up by them. Austin, however, puts forward the case for the feminist study of plays as follows:

> There are advantages for the feminist critical project of studying plays. Plays allow the reader and audience to visualize, to fill in blanks and gaps. They provide the frameworks for productions that can bring out many of the issues feminism finds pressing. They combine verbal and nonverbal elements simultaneously, so that questions of language and visual representation can be addressed at the same time, through the medium of an actual body.
>
> (1990: 2–3)

The object of Austin's own study is to apply feminist theory from different fields to re-read plays which, for the most part, are selected from the American 'canon'. This case study proposes a reversal of this activity: the plays, in this instance feminist theatre texts which are outside the 'canon', are presented as offering their own theoretical and critical field of feminism which other spheres of feminist activity 'find pressing'. The two plays under consideration are *Blood and Ice* by Liz Lochhead, and *Breathless* by April de Angelis which perform feminist re-inscriptions of Romanticism. They embody a number of the issues which concern feminist approaches to Romanticism in the fields of literary and cultural studies.

This final case study is offered as a conclusion to this present survey of feminism and theatre studies to suggest how, in a future phase of cross-disciplinary feminist activity, women's studies may look to the field of feminist theatre as a valuable source of critical practice: as a medium which maps out its theoretical and critical concerns on/through the body.

BLOOD AND ICE

Feminist literary approaches to the Romantic period have significantly challenged the definition and boundaries of what has been traditionally considered the Romantic canon. Readings of the 'male' canon have been re-framed by feminist theory and critical practice, and feminist scholarship has given attention to women writers marginalized by the canon. Mary Shelley is prominent among those women writers to have come to attention through this revisioning process. Lochhead's *Blood and Ice*, as a modern dramatization of the life and writing of Mary Shelley, makes many aspects of this feminist revisioning process visible in a performance context. *Blood and Ice*, like many of the feminist studies of Shelley, intertextually weaves the biographical text of Shelley's life with her fictional 'monsters' (see Mellor 1988). The dominant trope of *Blood and Ice* is Mary's quest for her own story, which is emblematic of the feminist quest to find the 'lost' woman writer. The 'woman' and the 'writing' are imaged in Lochhead's opening scene set in *'the ghostly nursery'*, where *'Mary alone, in a cold circle of candlelight, is reading her Frankenstein, surrounded by packing cases and nightmare toys'* (Lochhead 1985: 83). It is an image which is repeated throughout the play; 'the ghostly nursery' is the 'space' in which Mary's memories, the piecing together of her story, unfold. Lochhead's notes on the stage history of the play make it clear that the 'entire play' takes place in Mary Shelley's 'consciousness' (118).

Feminist psychoanalytic approaches to Romantic texts and contexts have been central to re-reading and re-reframing the writings of this period. *Blood and Ice*, performed in Mary Shelley's consciousness, theatricalizes the 'lost' woman writer as the desiring subject. Case (1989a) explores three kinds of subject positions in work by modern women playwrights: the split self, the metonymically displaced subject, and the collective subject. Lochhead's Mary Shelley is an example of what Case characterizes as the metonymically displaced subject, in which the desiring subject cannot take up a single subject position. Mary's fractured subject positioning is registered in the recalling of memories, the shifting between childhood, adolescence, maturity, etc. This subject positioning links, as Case explains in her contextualizing of Lacanian theory, to the object position: the desiring subject experiences the displacement of the object of desire and metonymically makes a substitution for that lack. Mary's object of desire is her own story, but it is constantly being displaced by the claims and attachments others make on her. There is a moment, for example, in Act Two, when Claire Clairmont, Mary's step-sister and Byron's lover, triggers Mary's mind back to Switzerland, to a time the spectator has been shown in Act One, when Claire was young and happy with Byron. Lochhead's directions indicate Mary *'snapping back from then by sheer will'* (104). Mary's story is also displaced by the story of her mother: the feminist writer, Mary Wollstonecroft, metonymically represented in the pendant containing the image of her 'famous mama' which Mary wears about her throat. Byron, who is twice imaged *'flicking'* the pendant, points to Mary's displacement of her own story as a desiring woman, and woman writer.

The trope of Mary's displaced story reflects the liminal position of the woman writer in relation to the Romantic canon, but also refigures the position of the masculine, the Romantic Poet (see Mellor 1993). The poets Byron and Shelley are staged in Mary's story, but they are refused the position of constructing her as the feminine Other. In one particular moment, Lochhead intervenes in the gaze, and gestically alienates the masculine as Other in the female gaze. She dramatizes the incident recounted by Polidori in which Byron was said to have been reading from Coleridge's *Christabel*:

> when silence ensued, and Shelley, suddenly shrieking, and putting his hands to his head, ran out of the room with a candle. Threw water on his face, and after gave him ether. He was looking at Mrs. Shelley [Mary], and suddenly thought of a woman he had heard of who had eyes instead of nipples, which, taking hold of his mind, horrified him.
>
> (Polidori, quoted in Leask 1992: 57)

However, in Lochhead's staging, it is Mary and not Byron who authors the gaze:

MARY:
'Her lips were red, her looks were free,
Her locks were yellow as gold;
Her skin was as white as leprosy,
The Nightmare Life in Death was she,
Who thicks man's blood with cold.'
Shelley has fit of hysterics and hallucination, screams.
SHELLEY: Mary, stop. Don't look at me so. Mary! You're naked, Mary . . . cover yourself . . . your breasts! Eyes, Mary, you have eyes for nipples. Don't stare at me. Piercing. The eyes in your breasts are staring me down, piercing me to the very soul . . .

(Lochhead: 99)

The construction of Woman in the Romantic gaze of the masculine is deconstructed in the materialist practice of *Blood and Ice*. In particular, Lochhead offers a materialist–feminist critique of motherhood, and highlights the realities and dangers of childbirth which dominated Mary Shelley's life given her mother's death as a result of birthing Mary, her own miscarriages, the deaths of her children, and so on. Lochhead dramatizes these as 'real' concerns for women and critically juxtaposes them with the Romantic poet's worship of 'Woman' and 'Motherhood':

SHELLEY: Mary, Woman is the door to all life. I sink to my knees and worship at her –
MARY: God save all women from men who worship 'Woman'.

(113)

'Woman worship' in the Romantic period, as materialist-feminist critic Mary Poovey describes, created 'contradictions between women's real needs and the increasingly idealized image of femininity' (1984: 30). The suturing of the 'proper lady' is imaged in Mary's dream, narrated to Shelley, which brings together a number of anxieties: of sexual jealousy, identity, repressed desire, self-denial, etc. In the dream, Mary sees Elise stitching a 'doll, a life-size puppet':

it was spread out here on the couch, long pale limbs, cadaver-loins gleaming whitely. Its dress was over its head, Claire-flounces turned inside out covering the whole top half of its body. And Elise was stitching. 'Long secret sutures,' she said, she spoke it out loud. 'A la victime is à la mode for all time, is it ?' And she smiled to herself. 'How shall I make her perfect. How shall I make her whole.' And she took my mother's book. 'Mary Wollstonecraft's Pattern Book' she said, 'Hints on the stitching up and finishing of ladies.' 'Satin stitch, French hemming, blanket stitch, and I'll finish with a strong knot where I join between the thighs lest it shall unravel,' and she bent down and bit off the end of the cotton with a snap.

(Lochhead 1985: 114)

The suturing imagery echoes Frankenstein's making of a 'man-made monster' in Shelley's story (see Mellor 1988: 38). In the dream imagery, it is the female body which is stitched up, made monstrous in the representational frame of Woman, which refuses the possibility of woman as desiring subject, and woman who in creating, birthing, faces death.

Lochhead stages the violence of the Romantic gaze on the female performer's body. For example, Claire wears a red velvet ribbon around her neck, the '*à la victime*' of the French Revolution, which images a suturing between head and body. In the 'mirror scene' of Act One, which is recalled in Act Two, Claire's body is laced into a 'filmy petticoat', the 'Claire-flounces' of Mary's dream, as she constructs herself as an object of male desire. Class-based oppression between women is also imaged through the body: specifically, Lochhead uses the device of the two-bodied doll to alienate class and gender:

> *She [Mary] is sadly toying with a doll, of a curiosity sort. It is a doll like Mary herself, clothed in her costume with hair in the colour and style of the actress who has the 'Mary' role. Under the skirt of the doll . . . is actually not the lower half of a body but another top half, that of a doll with the head, hairstyle and costume of the actress who is to play Elise. The skirt of this doll turns inside out and on the underside is doll-Elise's skirt, which will cover doll-Mary's head.*
>
> (103)

The doll images Mary's oppression of Elise: 'To be born poor is to be born a slave. To be born a woman is to be born a slave. Poor Elise, you were a slave's slave' (114).

In short, Lochhead's re-discovery of Mary Shelley as a woman writer, her critique of the Romantic poet, and her de-mythologization of the Romantic ideal of 'Woman', perform a criticism which makes visible several of the concepts and issues pre-occupying feminist studies of Romanticism in related fields.

BREATHLESS

Feminist readings of Shelley's *Frankenstein* frequently make reference to the traditions of Gothic fiction. Studies of Gothic fiction by feminist critics have been particularly concerned with the female-authored Gothic. Modelski has observed how the female Gothic can be used to express 'women's most intimate fears, or, more precisely, their fears about intimacy' (1990 [1982]: 20). 'Furthermore,' Modelski states, 'female Gothics provide an outlet for women's fears about fathers and husbands.' Mellor echoes this view by arguing the attraction of the Gothic for female writers on the grounds that 'its conventions permit them to explore one of the most deeply repressed experiences in a patriarchal culture, female sexual desire' (1988: 55). 'The medieval ruined castle or abbey,' Mellor continues, acted as 'a metaphor for the female body, penetrated by a sexually attractive villain' (ibid.). On the other hand, feminist analysis of male-authored Gothic fiction has highlighted the oppressive patriarchal discourse which seeks to control and repress female desire: 'the Gothic novel written by men presents the father's incestuous rape of his daughter as the perverse desire of the older generation to usurp the sexual rights of the younger generation' (197).

Breathless by April de Angelis is characterized as a 'gothic tale in one act', and performs a feminist criticism of the generic conventions and ideological discourses of the Gothic, in a way which both alienates the repressive patriarchal discourse of the male Gothic, and makes visible the 'gap' of the female Gothic in which female desire is staged. The action of *Breathless* is shared between Minna who role-plays the persecuted Gothic heroine, and Magda who role-plays her 'servant'. The role-playing of Gothic stereotypes is an important critical distancing technique. The actresses playing the roles do not 'become' them, but are metatheatrically alienated from them and the values which are inscribed in the construction of the female stereotypes. Furthermore, the setting of the Gothic which figures the female body as described above, is reversed in *Breathless*, where the performer's body is used to figure the setting. Minna, for example, role-playing the Gothic heroine à la Radcliffe, parodies the terror of the setting for the heroine as follows:

> All of a sudden amid the grim shadows Emily espied an ancient doorway. (*Minna feigns surprise*) Her hand, so delicate, so pale, reached out ... (*Minna's hand reaches out ...*)
> The door swung open! Its age-old hinges emitting a ghastly creak. (*Minna creaking*) Trembling ... almost fainting with horror, Emily had yet sufficient command to gather the feeble remains of her spirit and check the shriek that was escaping from her lips before ... dropping senseless to the floor! (*Minna drops*)
>
> (De Angelis 1990 [1986]: 71)

The shared role-playing between the two female characters constructs them as a 'collective subject'. Case, quoting from *Writing Beyond the Ending* by DuPlessis, explains this subject as 'a kind of transpersonal protagonist', made up of characters who represent a 'compendia of typical traits' and who establish 'a dialogue with habitual structures of satisfaction, ranges of feeling, and response' (1989a: 143). Magda and Minna establish 'a dialogue with the habitual structures' of the Gothic. They take on, cast off, and play with the 'typical traits' of the female servant and persecuted heroine. Their dialogue with the Gothic is playful and transgressive to make visible woman as a desiring subject.

In order for the female subject to take up a subject rather than object position in the Gothic frame, Minna and Magda have to take control of their own bodies and their own desires which patriarchal authority has denied them. Through role-playing they alienate the ways in which the female body is an object of male control in order to refuse the authority of the 'Father'. For example, *Breathless* demonstrates the dangers to women of male-controlled science and medicine. Minna, entering the discourse of the learned male medic, gives a 'lecture' on the female body. Her address on the male control of the female reproductive system is simultaneously performed on the body of Magda who is finally seen to *'crumple, slowly, in pain'* (77).

When role-playing the Gothic heroine, Minna is constructed as female hysteric. Clément explains the 'repressive' siting of this figure in the symbolic system as follows:

> the history of the hysteric ... takes place in half-confinement; the hysteric, dolefully reclining, tended and surrounded by doctors and worried family, is a prisoner inside the family; or else, in crisis, she bears the brunt of producing a medical spectacle.
>
> (Cixous and Clément 1987: 8)

In the role of hysteric, Minna's body is authored as a spectacle of male control, kept in her room in 'half-confinement':

> There are arms in soft cloth pushing me down they are like moths beating about my face and stifling me all I can think is how much my stays are biting me
> and how hard it is to
> take a breath
> Then it is quiet
> Another day
> Everyone goes quietly past Minna's room
>
> (De Angelis 1990 [1986]: 81)

149

Magda, as the female servant who serves the patriarch/scientist, is similarly repressed and imprisoned, both by her gender and her class, which deny her the opportunity to participate in the scientific field.

However, the rejection of their dual imprisonment is signalled in the final playing out and casting off of these two male-authored roles. The last exchange between Minna and Magda recites the ritual killing of the patriarch through Magda's narrative of women as the first, the ancient scientists, and Minna's simultaneous narrative which casts off the 'breathless' persecuted heroine Emily, for a woman who can walk out, alone, and breathing.

Like Lochhead's *Blood and Ice*, *Breathless* is able to make visible concepts which concern feminist studies of the Gothic/ Romanticism in 'sister' disciplines. Furthermore, it may be argued that *Breathless*, which en-acts the destruction of Father Law and proposes the birth of women's creativity, is emblematic of the feminist project which, broadly speaking, seeks to challenge and critique male dominance.

It still remains, however, for a future phase of women's studies to acknowledge the value of the 'new field theory' of feminist theatre studies for its critique of the 'breathless' realm of the 'masculine', and its capacity for representing the independent, 'breathing' woman as desiring subject.

BIBLIOGRAPHY

The first date is that of the edition cited in the text. The date of the first publication is given in square brackets. If the context requires it, both dates are given in the text as well.

Aston, E. (1986) 'Feminism and the French Theatre: A Turn-of-the-Century Perspective', *New Theatre Quarterly*, 7: 237–42.
—— (1988) 'Male Impersonation in the Music Hall: the Case of Vesta Tilley', *New Theatre Quarterly*, 15: 247–57.
—— (1989) *Sarah Bernhardt: A French Actress on the English Stage*, Oxford, New York, and Munich: Berg.
—— (1992a) 'The "New Woman" at Manchester's Gaiety Theatre', in V. Gardner and S. Rutherford (eds) *The New Woman and her Sisters: Feminism and Theatre 1850–1914*, New York and London: Harvester Wheatsheaf, 205–220.
—— (1992b) 'Ristori's Medea and her Nineteenth Century Successors', *Women and Theatre Occasional Papers*, 1: 38–47.
—— (1993a) 'Finding a Voice: Feminism and Theatre in the 1970s', in B. Moore-Gilbert (ed.) *The Arts in the 1970s: Cultural Closure?*, London and New York: Routledge, 99–128.
—— (1993b) 'Girls on Stage: Contemporary British Women's Theatre and the Teenage Question', *Modernes Theater*, 8: 153–63.
—— (1994) '"Meeting the Outside": The Theatre of Susan Glaspell', in G. Griffin (ed.) *Difference in View: Women and Modernism*, London: Falmer, 155–67.
Aston, E. and Griffin, G. (1991a) *Herstory: Volume 1*, Sheffield: Sheffield Academic Press.
—— (1991b) *Herstory: Volume 2*, Sheffield: Sheffield Academic Press.
Aston, E. and Savona, G. (1991) *Theatre as Sign-system: A Semiotics of Text and Performance*, London and New York: Routledge.
Austin, G. (1989) 'The Exchange of Women and Male Homosocial Desire in Arthur Miller's *Death of a Salesman* and Lilian Hellman's *Another Part of the Forest*', in J. Schlueter (ed.) *Feminist Readings of Modern American Drama*, London and Toronto: Associated University Press, 57–66.
—— (1990) *Feminist Theories for Dramatic Criticism*, Ann Arbor: University of Michigan Press.

Bamber, L. (1982) *Comic Women, Tragic Men: A Study of Gender and Genre in Shakespeare*, Stanford, California: Stanford University Press.

—— (1986) 'The Woman Reader in *King Lear*', in S. Barnet (ed.) (1987) *The Signet Classic Shakespeare: King Lear*, New York: Signet, 291–300.

Barker, C. (1994) 'What Training for What Theatre?', forthcoming, *New Theatre Quarterly*.

Barthes, R. (1977 [1966]) 'Structural Analysis of Narratives', in S. Heath (ed. and trans.) *Image, Music, Text*, London: Fontana, 79–124.

Bassi, K. (1989) 'The Actor as Actress in Euripides' *Alcestis*', in J. Redmond (ed.) *Themes in Drama: Women in Theatre: Volume II*, Cambridge: Cambridge University Press, 19–30.

Bassnett, S. (1980) 'Introduction to Theatre Semiotics', *Theatre Quarterly*, 38: 47–53.

—— (1984) 'Towards a Theory of Women's Theatre', in H. Schmid and A. Van Kesteren (eds) *Semiotics of Drama and Theatre: LLSEE, Volume 10*, Amsterdam and Philadelphia: John Benjamin, 445–66.

—— (1989a) *Magdalena: International Women's Experimental Theatre*, Oxford, New York, and Munich: Berg.

—— (1989b) 'Struggling with the Past: Women's Theatre in Search of a History', *New Theatre Quarterly*, 18: 107–12.

Beechy, V. (ed.) (1982) *The Changing Experience of Women: Unit One*, Milton Keynes: Open University Press.

Belsey, C. (1980) *Critical Practice*, London and New York: Methuen.

—— (1991 [1985]) *The Subject of Tragedy: Identity and Difference in Renaissance Drama*, London and New York: Routledge.

Benmussa, S. (1979) *The Singular Life of Albert Nobbs*, in *Benmussa Directs*, London: John Calder, 75–121; production notes, 22–26; production notes to Benmussa's *Portrait of Dora*, 9–19.

Ben-Zvi, L. (1986) 'Susan Glaspell and Eugene O'Neill: The Imagery of Gender', *Eugene O'Neill Newsletter*, 10(7): 22–7.

—— (1989) 'Susan Glaspell's Contributions to Contemporary Women Playwrights', in E. Brater (ed.) *Feminine Focus*, New York and Oxford: Oxford University Press, 147–66.

Berger, J. (1972) *Ways of Seeing*, Harmondsworth: Penguin.

Bernikow, L. (ed.) (1979 [1974]) *The World Split Open: Four Centuries of Women Poets in England and America, 1552–1950*, London: The Women's Press.

Bigsby, C. (ed.) (1987) *File on Miller*, London and New York: Methuen.

Boal, A. (1979) *Theatre of the Oppressed*, trans. C. A. and M. L. McBride, London: Pluto Press.

Brater, E. (ed.) (1989) *Feminine Focus*, New York and Oxford: Oxford University Press.

Bratton, J. S. (1992) 'Irrational Dress', in V. Gardner and S. Rutherford (eds) *The New Woman and her Sisters: Feminism and Theatre 1850–1914*, New York and London: Harvester Wheatsheaf, 77–91.

Braun, E. (1982) *The Director and the Stage: From Naturalism to Grotowski*, London: Methuen.

Brewster, Y. (ed.) (1987) *Black Plays*, New York and London: Methuen.

—— (ed.) (1989) *Black Plays: Two*, London and Portsmouth, New Hampshire: Methuen.

—— (1991) 'Drawing the Black and White Line: Defining Black Women's Theatre: The Director of Talawa Theatre in Interview', *New Theatre Quarterly*, 28: 361–8.

Brown, J. (1979) *Feminist Drama: Definition and Critical Analysis*, Metuchen, New Jersey and London: Scarecrow Press.

Browne, E. M. (1960) (ed.) *Eugene O'Neill: Anna Christie and Other Plays*, Harmondsworth: Penguin.

Butler, J. (1990) *Gender Trouble: Feminism and the Subversion of Identity*, London and New York: Routledge.

Butler, M. M. (1960) *Hrotsvitha: The Theatricality of her Plays* (New York: Philosophical Library.

Campbell, K. K. (1973) 'The Rhetoric of Women's Liberation: An Oxymoron', *Quarterly Journal of Speech*, 53: 74–86.

Caplan, B. (1991) 'Zofia Kalinska and the Demonic Woman: Work in Progress', in C. Robson (ed.) *Seven Plays by Women: Female Voices, Fighting Lives*, London: Aurora Metro, 15–18.

Case, S.-E. (1983) 'Re-Viewing Hrotsvit', *Theatre Journal*, 35: 533–42.

—— (1985) 'Classic Drag: The Greek Creation of Female Parts', *Theatre Journal*, 37: 317–27.

—— (1988) *Feminism and Theatre*, London: Macmillan.

—— (1989a) 'From Split Subject to Split Britches', in E. Brater (ed.) *Feminine Focus*, New York and Oxford: Oxford University Press, 126–46.

—— (1989b) 'Toward a Butch-Femme Aesthetic', in L. Hart, *Making a Spectacle: Feminist Essays on Contemporary Women's Theatre*, Ann Arbor: University of Michigan Press, 282–99.

—— (ed.) (1990) *Performing Feminisms: Feminist Critical Theory and Theatre*, Baltimore and London: Johns Hopkins University Press.

—— (1991) 'The Power of Sex: English Plays by Women, 1958–1988', *New Theatre Quarterly*, 27: 238–45.

Castrillo, C. (1992) 'The Exercising of Theatre Direction', *Magdalena Newsletter*, 7: 3.

Champagne, L. (ed.) (1990) *Out From Under: Texts by Women Performance Artists*, New York: Theatre Communications Group.

Churchill, C. (1977) in A. McFerran, 'Interview with Eight Women Playwrights', *Time Out*, 28 Oct–3 Nov: 13–15.

—— (1983) *Fen*, London: Methuen.

—— (1984 [1982]) *Top Girls*, London and New York: Methuen.

—— (1985 [1978]) *Vinegar Tom*, in *Churchill Plays: One*, London and New York: Methuen, 127–79.

—— (1985 [1979]) *Cloud Nine*, in *Churchill Plays: One*, London and New York: Methuen, 242–320.

Cixous, H. (1979) *Portrait of Dora*, in *Benmussa Directs*, London: John Calder, 28–67.

—— (1981 [1975]) 'The Laugh of the Medusa', trans. K. and P. Cohen, in E. Marks and I. de Courtivron (eds) *New French Feminisms*, Brighton: Harvester Press, 245–64.

—— (1984) 'Aller à la mer', trans. B. Kerslake, *Modern Drama*, 4: 546–8.
Cixous, H. and Clément, C. (1987 [1975]) *The Newly Born Woman*, trans.
  B. Wing, Manchester: Manchester University Press.
Clarke, I. (1992) 'Making Mrs Ebbsmith Notorious: Mrs Patrick Campbell
  as Agnes Ebbsmith', *Women and Theatre Occasional Papers*, 1: 48–62.
Cotton, N. (1980) *Women Playwrights in England: c. 1363–1750*, London and
  Toronto: Associated University Presses.
Coward, R. (1982) 'Sexual Violence and Sexuality', *Feminist Review*,
  11: 9–22.
—— (1984) *Female Desire: Women's Sexuality To-day*, London: Paladin.
Daniels, S. (1984) *Masterpieces*, London and New York: Methuen.
Davis, J. (ed.) (1987) *Lesbian Plays*, London and New York: Methuen.
—— (ed.) (1989) *Lesbian Plays: Two*, London and Portsmouth, New
  Hampshire: Methuen.
Davis, T. (1991) *Actresses as Working Women: Their Social Identity in
  Victorian Culture*, London and New York: Routledge.
Davy, K. (1986) 'Constructing the Spectator: Reception, Context, and
  Address in Lesbian Performance', *Performing Arts Journal*, 29: 43–52.
—— (1989) 'Reading Past the Heterosexual Imperative: *Dress Suits to
  Hire*', *The Drama Review*, 33: 153–70.
De Angelis, A. (1990 [1986]) *Breathless*, in F. Gray (ed.) *Second Wave Plays:
  Women at the Albany Empire*, Sheffield: Sheffield Academy Press, 67–83.
De Lauretis, T. (1984) *Alice Doesn't: Feminism Semiotics Cinema*, Bloom-
  ington: Indiana University Press.
—— (1987) *Technologies of Gender: Essays on Theory, Film, and Fiction*,
  Bloomington: Indiana University Press.
Deutsch, H. and Hanau, S. (1931) *The Provincetown: A Story of the Theatre*,
  New York: Russell & Russell.
Diamond, E. (1988) 'Brechtian Theory/Feminist Theory: Toward a Gestic
  Feminist Criticism', *The Drama Review*, 32: 82–94.
—— (1989) '(In)Visible Bodies in Churchill's Theater', in L. Hart (ed.)
  Making a Spectacle: Feminist Essays on Contemporary Women's Theatre,
  Ann Arbor: University of Michigan Press, 259–81.
—— (1990) 'Refusing the Romanticism of Identity: Narrative Inter-
  ventions in Churchill, Benmussa, Duras', in S. E. Case (ed.) *Performing
  Feminisms: Feminist Critical Theory and Theatre*, Baltimore and London:
  Johns Hopkins University Press, 92–105.
Doane, M. A. (1987) *The Desire to Desire: The Woman's Film of the 1940s*,
  London: Macmillan.
Dolan, J. (1984) 'Women's Theatre Program ATA: Creating a Feminist
  Forum', *Women and Performance*, 1(2): 5–13.
—— (1985a) 'Gender Impersonation Onstage: Destroying or Maintaining
  the Mirror of Gender Roles?', *Women and Performance*, 2(2): 5–11.
—— (1985b) 'Carmelita Tropicana Chats at the Club Chandalier', *The
  Drama Review*, 29: 26–32.
—— (1988) *The Feminist Spectator as Critic*, Ann Arbor: University of
  Michigan Press.
—— (1989a) 'Feminists, Lesbians, and Other Women in Theatre: Thoughts
  on the Politics of Performance', in J. Redmond (ed.) *Themes in Drama:*

Women in Theatre: Volume II, Cambridge: Cambridge University Press, 199–207.

—— (1989b) 'Desire Cloaked in a Trenchcoat', *The Drama Review*, 33: 59–67.

Dollimore, J. and Sinfield, A. (eds) (1985) *Political Shakespeare: New Essays in Cultural Materialism*, Manchester and New York: Manchester University Press.

Duffy, M. (1977) *The Passionate Shepherdess: Aphra Behn 1640–89*, London: Methuen.

Dunbar, A. (1988) *Three Stage Plays: Rita, Sue and Bob Too, with The Arbor and Shirley*, London and New York: Methuen.

Dunn, N. (1981) *Steaming*, Oxford: Amber Lane Press.

Dusinberre, J. (1975) *Shakespeare and the Nature of Women*, London: Macmillan.

Dworkin, A. (1981) *Pornography: Men Possessing Women*, London: The Women's Press.

Dymkowski, C. (1988) 'On the Edge: The Plays of Susan Glaspell', *Modern Drama*, 31: 91–105.

—— (1992) 'Entertaining Ideas: Edy Craig and the Pioneer Players', in V. Gardner and S. Rutherford (eds) *The New Woman and her Sisters: Feminism and Theatre 1850–1914*, New York and London: Harvester Wheatsheaf, 221–33.

Edgar, D. and Todd, S. (1979) *Teendreams*, London: Methuen.

Elam, K. (1988) 'Much Ado About Doing Things With Words (and Other Meanings): Some Problems in the Pragmatics of Theatre and Drama', in M. Issacharoff and R. F. Jones (eds) *Performing Texts*, Philadelphia: University of Pennsylvania Press, 39–58.

Féral, J. (1984) 'Writing and Displacement: Women in Theatre', trans. B. Kerslake, *Modern Drama*, 4: 549–63.

Ferris, L. (1990) *Acting Women*, London: Macmillan.

Fitzsimmons, L. (ed.) (1989) *File on Churchill*, London and Portsmouth, New Hampshire: Methuen.

Fitzsimmons, L. and Gardner, V. (eds) (1991) *New Woman Plays*, London and Portsmouth, New Hampshire: Methuen.

Flèche, A. (1989) '"A Monster of Perfection": O'Neill's "Stella"', in J. Schlueter (ed.) *Feminist Reading of Modern American Drama*, London and Toronto: Associated University Press, 25–36.

French, M. (1983 [1981]) *Shakespeare's Division of Experience*, London: Abacus.

Gale, M. (1988) 'Women Playwrights on the London Stage 1918–1939: Images of Women', unpublished M.A. thesis, University of Warwick.

Gardner, V. (ed.) (1985) *Sketches from the Actresses' Franchise League*, Nottingham: Nottingham Drama Texts.

Gardner, V. and Rutherford, S. (eds) (1992) *The New Woman and her Sisters: Feminism and Theatre 1850–1914*, New York and London: Harvester Wheatsheaf.

Gilder, R. (1931) *Enter the Actress: The First Women in the Theatre*, London, Bombay and Sydney: George G. Harrap.

Gillespie, P. P. (1978) 'Feminist Theatre: A Rhetorical Phenomenon', *The Quarterly Journal of Speech*, 64: 284–94.

Glaspell, S. (1987) *Plays by Susan Glaspell*, ed. C. W. E. Bigsby, Cambridge: Cambridge University Press.

Goldberg, I. (1922) *The Drama of Transition: Native and Exotic Playcraft*, Cincinnati: Stewart Kidd.

Goodman, L. (1993a) *Contemporary Feminist Theatres: To Each Her Own*, London and New York: Routledge.

—— (1993b) 'Feminist Theatre in Britain: A Survey and a Prospect', *New Theatre Quarterly*, 33: 66–84.

Gray, F. (ed.) (1990) *Second Wave Plays: Women at the Albany Empire*, Sheffield: Sheffield Academic Press.

Greenhalgh, J. (1992) 'The Magdalena Project', *Women and Theatre Occasional Papers*, 1: 107–10.

Griffin, G. (1991) 'Turning on the Mother: The Dramatization of Anxiety Concerning "the Mother" in Plays from the 1890s to the 1980s', *Modernes Theater*, 6(1): 25–40.

Hanna, G. (1978) *Feminism and Theatre*, Theatre Papers, 2nd series, no. 8, Dartington, Devon: Dartington College.

—— (1989) 'Writing our own History: Feminist Theatricals', *Trouble and Strife*, 16: 47–52.

—— (ed.) (1991) *Monstrous Regiment: Four Plays and a Collective Celebration*, London: Nick Hern.

Harriss K. (1989) 'New Alliances: Socialist-Feminism in the Eighties', *Feminist Review*, 31: 34–54.

Hart, L. (ed.) (1989) *Making a Spectacle: Feminist Essays on Contemporary Women's Theatre*, Ann Arbor: University of Michigan Press.

—— (1990) 'Canonizing Lesbians?', in J. Schlueter (ed.) *Modern American Drama: The Female Canon*, London and Toronto: Associated University Presses, 275–92.

Hartmann, H. (1979) 'The Unhappy Marriage of Marxism and Feminism: Towards a More Progressive Union', *Capital and Class*, 8: 1–33.

Helms, L. (1990) 'Playing the Woman's Part: Feminist Criticism and Shakespeare', in S. E. Case (ed.) *Performing Feminisms: Feminist Critical Theory and Theatre*, Baltimore and London, Johns Hopkins University Press, 196–206.

Holledge, J. (1981) *Innocent Flowers: Women in the Edwardian Theatre*, London: Virago.

Hood, S. (ed.) (1991) *A Woman Alone and Other Plays: Franca Rame and Dario Fo*, London: Methuen.

hooks, b. (1982) *Ain't I a Woman: Black Women and Feminism*, London: Pluto Press.

—— (1984) *Feminist Theory: From Margin to Center*, Boston: South End Press.

Howe, E. (1992) *The First English Actresses: Women and Drama 1660–1700*, Cambridge: Cambridge University Press.

Hrotsvit (1984) *Dulcitius*, trans. in K. M. Wilson (ed.) *Medieval Women Writers*, Manchester: Manchester University Press, 53–60.

Hughes, H. (1989a) 'Polymorphous Perversity and the Lesbian Scientist' interview, *The Drama Review*, 33: 171–83.
—— (1989b) *Dress Suits to Hire, The Drama Review*, 33: 132–52.
Innes, C. (1992) *Modern British Drama 1890–1990*, Cambridge: Cambridge University Press.
Irigaray, L. (1981 [1977]) 'This Sex Which Is Not One', trans. C. Reeder, in E. Marks and I. de Courtivron (eds) *New French Feminisms*, Brighton: Harvester Press, 99–110.
——(1985 [1974]) *Speculum of the Other Women*, Ithaca, New York: Cornell University Press.
——(1985 [1977]) *This Sex Which Is Not One*, Ithaca, New York: Cornell University Press.
—— (1993) *je, tu, nous: Toward a Culture of Difference*, trans. A. Martin, London and New York: Routledge.
Itzin, C. (1980) *Stages in the Revolution: Political Theatre in Britain Since 1968*, London: Methuen.
Jardine, L. (1989 [1983]) *Still Harping on Daughters: Women and Drama in the Age of Shakespeare*, 2nd edition, New York and London: Harvester Wheatsheaf.
Kaplan, E. A. (1983) *Women and Film: Both Sides of the Camera*, London and New York: Methuen.
Kappeler, S. (1986) *The Pornography of Representation*, Cambridge: Polity Press.
Kay, J. (1987) *Chiaroscuro*, in J. Davis (ed.) *Lesbian Plays*, London and New York: Methuen, 57–84.
Kent, C. (1980 [1977]) 'Image and Reality: The Actress and Society', in M. Vicinus (ed.) *A Widening Sphere: Changing Roles of Victorian Women*, London: Methuen, 94–116.
Keyssar, H. (1984) *Feminist Theatres*, London: Macmillan.
Kristeva, J. (1977) 'Modern Theater Does Not Take (a) Place', trans. in *Substance*, 18/19: 131–4.
—— (1980) *Desire in Language*, L. S. Roudiez (ed.), Oxford: Basil Blackwell.
—— (1982 [1979]) 'Women's Time', trans. A. Jardine and H. Blake, in N. O. Keohane, M. Z. Rosaldo, and B. C. Gelpi (eds) *Feminist Theory: A Critique of Ideology*, Brighton: Harvester Press, 31–53.
Lamont, R. C. (1989) 'The Reverse Side of a Portrait: The Dora of Freud and Cixous', in E. Brater (ed.) *Feminine Focus*, New York and Oxford: Oxford University Press, 79–93.
Larabee, A. E. (1990) 'Meeting the Outside Face to Face: Susan Glaspell, Djuna Barnes, and O'Neill's *The Emperor Jones*', in J. Schlueter (ed.) *Modern American Drama: The Female Canon*, London and Toronto: Associated Presses, 77–85.
Lavery, B. (1987) *Origin of the Species*, in M. Remnant (ed.) *Plays by Women: Volume Six*, London and New York: Methuen, 63–84.
Leask, N. (1992) 'Shelley's "Magnetic Ladies": Romantic Mesmerism and the Politics of the Body', in S. Copley and J. Whale (eds) *Beyond Romanticism*, London and New York: Routledge, 53–78.
Leavitt, D. L. (1980) *Feminist Theatre Groups*, Jefferson, North Carolina: McFarland & Co.

Lenz, C., Greene, G., and Neely, C. (eds) (1980) *The Woman's Part: Feminist Criticism of Shakespeare*, Urbana and Chicago: University of Illinois Press.

Levy, D. (1987) *Heresies*, in *Two Plays by Deborah Levy*, London: Methuen.

—— (1992) 'The Making of the B File', *Magdalena Newsletter*, 7: 2.

—— (1993) 'Questions of Survival: Towards a Postmodern Feminist Theatre', *New Theatre Quarterly*, 35: 225–30.

Lewisohn, L. (1920) 'Susan Glaspell', *The Nation*, 3 November, 509–10.

—— (1932) *Expression in America*, London: Thornton Butterworth.

Lochhead, L. (1985) *Blood and Ice*, in M. Wandor (ed.) *Plays for Women: Volume Four*, London and New York: Methuen, 81–118.

Lotman, J. H. (1979 [1973]) 'The Origin of Plot in the Light of Typology', trans. J. Graffy, *Poetics Today*, 1(1–2): 161–84.

Macpherson, J. (1989) 'Younger Women and Feminism', interview, *Feminist Review*, 31: 135–9.

Maitland, S. (1986) *Vesta Tilley*, London: Virago.

Marks, E. and I. de Courtivron (eds) (1981) *New French Feminisms*, Brighton: Harvester Press.

McDonald, J. (1986) *The 'New Drama' 1900–1914*, London: Macmillan.

Mcluskie K. (1985) 'The Patriarchal Bard: Feminist Criticism and Shakespeare: *King Lear* and *Measure for Measure*', in J. Dollimore and A. Sinfield (eds) *Political Shakespeare: New Essays in Cultural Materialism*, Manchester and New York, Manchester University Press, 88–108.

Mellor A. K. (1988) *Mary Shelley: Her Life Her Fiction Her Monsters*, London and New York: Routledge.

—— (1993) *Romanticism and Gender*, London and New York: Routledge.

Miles, J. (ed.) (1986) *Women Heroes: Six Short Plays from the Women's Project*, New York: Applause.

Miller, A. (1961 [1949]) *Death of a Salesman*, Harmondsworth: Penguin.

Millett, K. (1977 [1969]) *Sexual Politics*, London: Virago.

Mitchell, J. and Rose, J. (eds) (1982) *Feminine Sexuality: Jacques Lacan and the école freudienne*, London: Macmillan.

Modelski, T. (1990 [1982]) *Loving with a Vengeance: Mass-produced Fantasies for Women*, London and New York: Routledge.

—— (1991) *Feminism Without Women: Culture and Criticism in a 'Post-feminist' Age*, London and New York: Routledge.

Moers, E. (1976) *Literary Women*, New York: Doubleday.

Moi, T. (1985) *Sexual/Textual Politics: Feminist Literary Theory*, London and New York: Methuen.

Moore, H. (ed.) (1977) *The New Women's Theatre: Ten Plays by Contemporary Women*, New York: Vintage Books.

Morgan, F. (ed.) (1981) *The Female Wits: Women Playwrights of the Restoration*, London: Virago.

Morgan, F. and Lyons, P. (eds) (1991) *Female Playwrights of the Restoration: Five Comedies*, London: Dent.

Mulvey, L. (1975) 'Visual Pleasure and Narrative Cinema', *Screen*, 16(3): 6–18.

Natalle, E. (1985) *Feminist Theatre: A Study in Persuasion*, Metuchen, New Jersey and London: Scarecrow Press.

Nelson, D. (1982) 'O'Neill's Women', *Eugene O'Neill Newsletter*, 6(2): 3–7.

Nichols, G. (1990a [1983]) *i is a long memoried woman*, London: Karnak.

Novak, S. S. (1972) 'The Invisible Woman: The Case of the Female Playwright in German Literature', *Journal of Social Issues*, 28(2): 47–57.

Ozieblo, B. (1990) 'Rebellion and Rejection: The Plays of Susan Glaspell', in J. Schlueter (ed.) *Modern American Drama: The Female Canon*, London and Toronto: Associated University Press, 66–76.

Page, L. (1982) *Tissue*, in M. Wandor (ed.) *Plays by Women: Volume One*, London and New York: Methuen, 75–104.

Parmar, P. (1989) 'Other Kinds of Dreams', *Feminist Review*, 31: 55–65.

Pasquier, M. C. (1986) 'Women in the Theatre of Men: What Price Freedom?', in J. Friedlander, B. Wiesen Cook, A. Kessler-Harris, and C. Smith-Rosenberg (eds) *Women in Culture and Politics: A Century of Change*, Bloomington: Indiana University Press, 194–206.

Pavis, P. (1985) 'Theatre Analysis: Some Questions and a Questionnaire', *New Theatre Quarterly*, 2: 208–12.

Plath, S. (1981 [1962]) *Three Women: A Poem for Three Voices*, in T. Hughes (ed.) *Collected Poems*, London and Boston: Faber & Faber.

Poovey, M. (1984) *The Proper Lady and the Woman Writer*, Chicago and London: University of Chicago Press.

Propp, V. (1968 [1928]) *Morphology of the Folktale*, trans. and revised edition, Austin and London: University of Texas Press.

Quinn, A. H. (1927) *A History of the American Drama: From the Civil War to the Present Day*, New York and London: Harper.

Radel, N. F. (1990) 'Provincetown Plays: Women Writers and O'Neill's American Intertext', *Essays in Theatre*, 9(1): 31–43.

Rawlence, C. (1980) Introduction to *Strike While the Iron is Hot*, in M. Wandor (ed.) *Strike While the Iron is Hot: Three Plays on Sexual Politics*, London and West Nyack: Journeyman Press, 17–19.

Rea, C. (1972) 'Women's Theatre Groups', *The Drama Review*, 16: 79–89.

Redmond, J. (ed.) (1989) *Themes in Drama: Women in Theatre: Volume II*, Cambridge: Cambridge University Press.

Reinelt (1990) 'Beyond Brecht: Britain's New Feminist Drama', in S. E. Case (ed.) *Performing Feminisms: Feminist Critical Theory and Theatre*, Baltimore and London: Johns Hopkins University Press, 150–9.

Reinelt, J. G. and Roach, J. R. (1992) *Critical Theory and Performance*, Ann Arbor: University of Michigan Press.

Reinhardt, N. S. (1981) 'New Directions for Feminist Criticism in Theatre and the Related Arts', in E. Langland and W. Gore (eds), *A Feminist Perspective in the Academy: The Difference it Makes*, Chicago: University of Chicago Press.

Remnant, M. (ed.) (1986) *Plays by Women: Volume Five*, London and New York: Methuen.

—— (ed.) (1987) *Plays by Women: Volume Six*, London and New York: Methuen.

Robson, C. (ed.) (1991) *Seven Plays by Women: Female Voices, Fighting Lives*, London: Aurora Metro.

Roudiez, L. S. (1980) 'Introduction', in J. Kristeva, *Desire in Language*, Oxford: Basil Blackwell, 1–20.

Rowbotham, S. (1973) *Hidden From History*, London: Pluto Press.

Rubin, G. (1975) 'The Traffic in Women: Notes on the "Political Economy" of Sex', in R. Reiter (ed.) *Toward an Anthropology of Women*, New York and London: Monthly Review Press, 157–210.

Rudet, J. (1986) *Money to Live*, in M. Remnant (ed.) *Plays by Women: Volume Five*, London and New York: Methuen, 145–81.

—— (1987) *Basin*, in V. Brewster (ed.) *Black Plays*, New York and London: Methuen, 113–39.

Running-Johnson, C. (1989) 'Feminine Writing and its Theatrical "Other"', in J. Redmond (ed.) *Themes in Drama: Women in Theatre: Volume II*, Cambridge: Cambridge University Press, 177–83.

Rutter, C. (1988) *Clamorous Voices: Shakespeare's Women Today*, London: The Women's Press.

Savona, J. L. (1989) 'In Search of a Feminist Theater: *Portrait of Dora*', in E. Brater (ed.) *Feminist Focus*, New York and Oxford: Oxford University Press, 94–108.

Schlueter, J. (ed.) (1989) *Feminist Readings of Modern American Drama*, London and Toronto: Associated University Presses.

—— (ed.) (1990) *Modern American Drama: The Female Canon*, London and Toronto: Associated University Presses.

Sears, D. (1990) *Afrika Solo*, Toronto: Sister Vision.

Senelick, L. (1982) 'The Evolution of the Male Impersonator on the Nineteenth-century Popular Stage', *Essays in Theatre*, 1: 30–44.

Silverman, K. (1983) *The Subject of Semiotics*, New York: Oxford University Press.

Sinfield, A. (1985) 'Royal Shakespeare: Theatre and the Making of Ideology', in J. Dollimore and A. Sinfield (eds) *Political Shakespeare: New Essays in Cultural Materialism*, Manchester and New York: Manchester University Press, 158–81.

Solomon, A. (1985) 'The WOW Cafe', *The Drama Review*, 29: 92–101.

Speakman, D. (1991) 'The Next Stage: Devaluation, Revaluation, and After', in C. Robson (ed.) *Seven Plays by Women: Female Voices, Fighting Lives*, London: Aurora Metro, 19–25.

Spender, D. and Hayman, C. (eds) (1985) *How the Vote Was Won and Other Suffragette Plays*, London and New York: Methuen.

Stokes, J. (1992) 'Helena Modjeska in England', *Women and Theatre Occasional Papers*, 1: 19–37.

Stokes, J., Booth, M.R., and Bassnett, S. (1988) *Bernhardt, Terry, Duse: The Actress in her Time*, Cambridge: Cambridge University Press.

Stowell, S. (1992a) *A Stage of their Own: Feminist Playwrights of the Suffrage Era*, Manchester: Manchester University Press.

—— (1992b) 'Drama as Trade: Cicely Hamilton's *Diana of Dobson's*', in V. Gardner and S. Rutherford (eds) *The New Woman and her Sisters: Feminism and Theatre 1850–1914*, New York and London: Harvester Wheatsheaf, 177–88.

Taplin, O. (1985 [1978]) *Greek Tragedy in Action*, revised edition, London: Methuen.

Thompson, J. (1992) '"The World Made Flesh": Women and Theatre', in

A. Page (ed.) *The Death of the Playwright?*, London: Macmillan, 24–42.

Thomson, P. (1991) 'The First Drama Department?', *Studies in Theatre Production*, 3: 42.

Trewin, J. C. (1976) *The Edwardian Theatre*, Oxford: Basil Blackwell.

Trussler, S. (1986) 'Commentary on *The Rover*', Swan Theatre Plays series, London: Methuen.

Vorse, M. H. (1991 [1942]) *Time and the Town*, New Brunswick, New Jersey: Rutgers University Press.

Wakefield, L. and the Women's Theatre Group (1984) *Time Pieces*, in M. Wandor (ed.) *Plays by Women: Volume Three*, London and New York: Methuen, 125–61.

Wandor, M. (ed.) (1980) *Strike While the Iron is Hot: Three Plays on Sexual Politics*, London and West Nyack: Journeyman Press.

—— (ed.) (1982) *Plays by Women: Volume One*, London and New York: Methuen.

—— (ed.) (1984a) *Plays by Women: Volume Three*, London and New York: Methuen.

—— (1984b) 'The Impact of Feminism on the Theatre', *Feminist Review*, 18: 76–92.

—— (ed.) (1985) *Plays by Women: Volume Four*, London and New York: Methuen.

—— (1986 [1981]) *Carry on, Understudies: Theatre and Sexual Politics*, revised edition, London and New York: Routledge.

Waterman, A. (1966) *Susan Glaspell*, New York: Twayne.

Wertenbaker, T. (1989) *The Love of the Nightingale*, London: Faber & Faber.

Wheelwright, J. (1989) *Amazons and Military Maids*, London: Pandora.

Whitford, M. (ed.) (1991) *The Irigaray Reader*, Oxford: Basil Blackwell.

Willis, S. (1990) 'Hélène Cixous's *Portrait of Dora*: The Unseen and the Un-Scene', in S. E. Case (ed.) *Performing Feminisms: Feminist Critical Theory and Theatre*, Baltimore and London: Johns Hopkins University Press, 77–91.

Wilson, K. M. (ed.) (1984) *Medieval Women Writers*, Manchester: Manchester University Press.

Women's Theatre Group and Feinstein, E. (1991) *Lear's Daughters*, in E. Aston and G. Griffin (Eds) *Herstroy: Volume 1*, Sheffield: Sheffield Academic Press, 19–69.

Woodfield, J. (1984) *English Theatre in Transition 1881–1914*, London: Croom Helm.

Yarbro-Bejarano, Y. (1990) 'The Female Subject in Chicano Theatre: Sexuality, "Race," and Class', in S. E. Case (ed.) *Performing Feminisms: Feminist Critical Theory and Theatre*, Baltimore and London: Johns Hopkins University Press, 131–49.

Zeig, S. (1985) 'The Actor as Activator: Deconstructing Gender Through Gesture', *Women and Performance*, 2(2), 12–17.

Zhana (ed.) (1988) *Sojourn*, London: Methuen.

Zivanovic, J. (1989) 'The Rhetorical and Political Foundations of Women's Collaborative Theatre', in J. Redmond (ed.) *Themes in Drama: Women in Theatre: Volume II*, Cambridge: Cambridge University Press, 209–19.

INTRODUCTION TO FEMINISM AND THEATRE
INTERVIEWS (UNPUBLISHED)

Monstrous Regiment (1990): Chris Bowler, Gillian Hanna, and Mary McCusker.
Siren Theatre Company (1989): Jane Boston and Jude Winter.
Spare Tyre Theatre Company (1989): Clair Chapman, Katina Noble, and Harriet Powell.
Women and Theatre (1989): Jo Broadwood, Lorna Laidlaw, and Norma Morris.
Women's Theatre Group (1989): Adjoa Andoh, Jenny Clarke, Jacqueline Francis, Mary Jeremiah, Deb'bora John-Wilson, Hazel Maycock, Alison Mckinnon, and Greta Millington.
Women's Theatre Group (1990): Jenny Clarke and Claire Grove.

RECORDED MATERIAL

Blood and Wine: The Poetry and Prose of Amryl Johnson (1991), tape cassette recording, Cofa Press.
i is a long memoried woman, G. Nichols (1990b), video cassette recording, A Leda Serena/Yod Production.
Fascinating Aïda (1992) interviewed in *The 'X' Factor* series, presented by Emma Freud, Radio 4, 1992.

CONFERENCES ON WOMEN'S THEATRE

'Transformations and Transpositions: Changing Patterns in Women's Theatre History', organized by Susan Bassnett, University of Warwick, 1985.
'Women's Theatre Festival and Conference', organized by Susan Triesman, University of Strathclyde, 1986.
'Gender – Text – Image: Women in Theatre: Twentieth Century Perspectives', organized by Elaine Aston, Nene College, 1988.
'Latchkeys and Cigarettes: The New Woman in British Theatre 1880–1914', organized by Viv Gardner, University of Manchester, 1989.
'Twentieth Century Perspectives on Women and Theatre: Creation, Process, Output', organized by Susan Bassnett and Maggie Gale, University of Warwick, 1990.
'Women, Herstory, and Theatre: Women's Theatrical Practice', organized by Elaine Aston, University of Loughborough, 1991.
'Archetype, Stereotype, Prototype: Women in Theatre', organized by Susan Bassnett and Maggie Gale, University of Warwick, 1992.

INDEX

163

INDEX